Praise for *The Walking Popsicle Stick*

Marilyn Johnson has woven together a delightful collection of true children's stories, each calculated to teach a specific character-building lesson. Using illustrations drawn from the natural world, she writes as an eyewitness to each interesting incident. She captures the joy and wonder of the children as they move from one experience to another.

~ Bill Krick, Literature Ministries Director

I love a story with a lesson. The author has successfully turned true life events into humorous, enduring lessons for all of us. Her true stories of life abroad, or on the farm with her young family, entertain as well as give us biblical truths. Her stories give us vivid descriptions of the events along with thoughts and conversations we can all relate to. As an animal lover, I appreciate the nature facts and loving attitude she displays in her writing, especially towards Squawky Cocky. These stories will endure from generation to generation. God's love and truth is evident throughout. Truly a pleasure to read and share with my kids.

~ Amy Merriam, Registered Dental Hygienist and Mother of Three

The stories in *The Walking Popsicle Stick* are attractive, engaging, and educational. They were so fun I didn't realize all the moral lessons I was learning. As a kid, I have enjoyed *The Walking Popsicle Stick*, and I am sure you will too. If you are looking for a solid, amazing book for your kids this is the book for you. I would recommend this book to anyone.

~ Iaroslav Lotca Puente, Student, Age 10

With an unusually deep cultural understanding, Marilyn Johnson has gathered from a goldmine of real experiences to create this book. Her unique, educational stories open our eyes to God's intriguing creatures and convey valuable life lessons for young and old.

~ Heather Krick, Home Schooling Mom

What a fun read for the whole family! You get to learn how amazing God's creatures are and how we can learn from them. Mrs. Johnson was the kindergarten class chaplain where I taught. The students were excited to hear her stories and were amazed by the many first-hand experiences she shared with us. She has a heart full of love for kids of all ages and wants each one to know Jesus as their best Friend!

~ Marla Rasmussen, Principal/Teacher

Parents, teachers, and anyone who loves to read or be read to, if you like great stories that involve animals and harrowing experiences, this book is for you. I highly recommend this book, and I can't say enough about how much I love the stories. Mernie is a gifted story teller and writer.

~ Teri Ann Ricchiuti, Middle School Teacher

The Walking Popsicle Stick
and Other Nature Stories

Marilyn "Mernie" Johnson

World rights reserved. This book or any portion thereof may not be copied or reproduced in any form or manner whatever, except as provided by law, without the written permission of the publisher, except by a reviewer who may quote brief passages in a review.

The author assumes full responsibility for the accuracy of all facts and quotations as cited in this book. The opinions expressed in this book are the author's personal views and interpretations, and do not necessarily reflect those of the publisher.

This book is provided with the understanding that the publisher is not engaged in giving spiritual, legal, medical, or other professional advice. If authoritative advice is needed, the reader should seek the counsel of a competent professional.

Copyright © 2024 Marilyn Johnson
Copyright © 2024 TEACH Services, Inc.
ISBN-13: 978-1-4796-1793-7 (Paperback)
ISBN-13: 978-1-4796-1794-4 (ePub)
Library of Congress Control Number: 2024910530

Scripture quotations marked ERV are taken from The Holy Bible, Easy-to-Read Version, Copyright © 2006 by Bible League International.

Scripture quotations marked GW are taken from The Holy Bible, GOD'S WORD Translation, Copyright © 1995, 2003, 2013, 2014, 2019, 2020 by God's Word to the Nations Mission Society. All rights reserved.

Scripture quotations marked ICB are taken from The Holy Bible, International Children's Bible®, Copyright© 1986, 1988, 1999, 2015 by Thomas Nelson. Used by permission.

Scripture quotations marked NIRV are taken from The Holy Bible, New International Reader's Version, Copyright © 1995, 1996, 1998, 2014 by Biblica, Inc.®. Used by permission. All rights reserved worldwide.

Scripture quotations marked NIV are taken from The Holy Bible, New International Version®, NIV® Copyright ©1973, 1978, 1984, 2011 by Biblica, Inc.® Used by permission. All rights reserved worldwide.

www.TEACHServices.com • (800) 367-1844

Dedication

To Snicki, my reason and inspiration for writing this book,

and to each one of my grandchildren.

Table of Contents

Acknowledgments ix
Welcome to Our Zoo 11
    Poem: My Zoo 12
The Walking Popsicle Stick 14
    Poem: Look at the Ant 18
No Entry: Camels Only 19
    Poem: The Grumbler 23
Starfish and Broken Arms 24
    Poem: Keep Trying 28
Adapa-what? 29
    Poem: Stay Happy 32
Oh, Rats! 33
Dirty Helpers 37
    Poem: Happy Helpers 41
The Deadly Beauty 43
    Poem: True Beauty 47
The Hidden Destroyers 49
    Poem: The Spoilers 53
Don't Be a Chameleon! 54
    Poem: Just Be Yourself 59
Monkey See, Monkey Do 60
    Poem: Copycat 64

Trapped!..65
  Poem: Beware!..70
The Voice of Instinct...71
  Poem: The Little Voice..74
The Kay-Nines...75
  Poem: Loyalty...80
Squawky Cocky..81
Acey's Gift..87
Sweet or Stinky?..91
Where Are You?..96
The Crawling Carpet..101
  Poem: Look for the Rainbow.. 104
The Silvery Trail Makers...107
  Poem: Your Trail.. 109
Thief in the Night...110

Acknowledgments

Thank you …

… to each of my children, for making life interesting with all the animals that have walked, crawled, swum, or flown through our lives;

… to Grandma Johnson, for the many, many nature books and magazines she gave us through the years;

… to Alyssa, for patiently helping me edit the stories, for her loyalty and love in rating every one of Grandma's stories a 10 out of 10, and for wondering what else she could do to help;

… to all the others who have helped with editing;

… and to all our friends, whose lives have added interesting stories to this book.

Welcome to Our Zoo

Hi! I'm Mrs. Johnson – but in this book I'm "Mama" – and I want to welcome you to my family's zoo! The stories you are about to read are just some of the whole Johnson family's adventures with nature. Some of them happened in America, but many are from other countries. We lived and travelled in Asia for thirty years, so you'll find stories from Singapore, Malaysia, Thailand, Pakistan, and India.

I know you will be surprised by some of the stories, and I'm pretty sure you will learn interesting facts about many animals. How do Mama and Daddy know so much about nature? We have spent a lot of time reading nature books and magazines.

Also, after you read a few of the stories in this book, you might wonder if they could possibly have happened. A friend who read the manuscript, when asked the same question, answered that no one could possibly make up the wilder events in these stories. In short, the answer to the question is *yes*, the hardest to believe really did happen!

Actually, I realize that I didn't write about when Daddy and I went to a zoo in Afghanistan, so I'll tell that story now. As we were walking along side by side, all of a sudden I felt something taking hold of my right hand. But it wasn't Daddy – he was on the other side of me. Imagine my surprise when I looked and saw that it was a big hairy gorilla!

You might also wonder how any family could have so many aunts and uncles. The truth is that our biological family really doesn't include many aunts and uncles at all. However, remember that these events happened in several different countries on different continents, and that in some of those places, it is good manners to call your parents' friends "Auntie" and "Uncle."

Finally, in some of the stories, I have used people's real names. In others, I've given them different ones. But all of the animals are called by their real names!

Now you know, so jump right in and enjoy our animal adventures!

☙ ❖ ❧

My Zoo

My house is sort of like a zoo
With lovebirds, mynah and a cockatoo.
Besides my birds, on top of that,
I also have a little cat,
And thirteen hamsters – I started with two –
But when mothers give birth, what to do?
The cages are all in the room where we eat;
As I eat my meals, birds chirp and they tweet.
The hamsters are quiet, their noses just wiggle;
When they hang from their bars, then I start to giggle.
The cat sits outside and cries, "Me-ew,"
Wanting inside to eat with us, too.
The mynah – Rascal – hops around to say,
"I'd like some rice, please, right away!"
He barks like a dog, he whistles, and more …
He mimics the sound of a knock on the door.
And if we laugh while eating our food,
Rascal laughs too, as he catches our mood.
Cocky the cockatoo just sits on his perch
And squawks and begs while I go in search
Of some fruit or seeds that he'd like to eat …
Or nuts in the shell as a special treat.
Sometimes he likes me to scratch his neck,
While I just hope he won't bite or peck.
When I bought Goldilocks, with fur blondish-red,
"She's already pregnant," the storekeeper said.
Soon many hamsters were born to my "zoo."
I couldn't keep many, so what should I do?

If you want to know how that story ends …
I gave them away to all of my friends!
Mama used to say, "We can't have a cat,"
But our friends gave us one and took care of that!
'Migo sneaks in the house when I open the door;
He plays and he hides and he likes to explore.
He jumps on the table; he gets on my bed.
"That cat has no manners," my Daddy has said.
Yes, my house is sort of like a zoo;
With the lovebirds, mynah, and cockatoo,
With the cat and the hamsters, it's lots of fun,
And there's so much to learn from every one.
Though some are big, and some are quite small,
Each one is special, and I love them all!

The Walking Popsicle Stick

Rrrinnnngggggg! The school bell rang, and Chris was happy that classes were finally finished for the day. Quickly he loaded up his backpack and hurried out of the classroom. As he left the building, Chris waved and said goodbye to Danny, Joseph, and his other friends. Across the campus he walked until he reached the sidewalk, where he would turn to go toward his house, which was really, really close by.

Suddenly Chris noticed something very strange. He could hardly believe what was just in front of him: a popsicle stick crawling down the sidewalk. Wait, what?!

Chris blinked his eyes and looked again. It was true: the popsicle stick really was moving slowly, slowly down the walk. He stopped and watched for a while. Then he hurried on home.

When he got there, he dropped his backpack on the desk in his bedroom and quickly went to tell Mama, Emma and his little sister Danielle. "Guess what I saw on the way home!" he said excitedly.

"What?" Mama asked. "I'm curious!"

"A popsicle stick walking down the sidewalk," he told them.

"No way!" Emma said in disbelief.

"It's true," Chris said. "A lot of big red ants were working together trying to pull the stick back to their home. So the popsicle stick was moving right down the sidewalk."

"Ants are very interesting little insects," Mama answered.

"Interesting little what?" Danielle asked.

"Insects," Emma told her. "Ants are insects. I learned about them in science class at school. All insects have six legs, and they have three parts to their bodies. First is the head, which has big eyes, sharp jaws, and two antennae – "

"What are those?" Danielle asked.

"Antennae? They're feelers, for feeling and smelling," Emma told her. "Next comes the thorax, or chest. All the legs grow out from the thorax. The last part of the body is the abdomen."

"You're right, Emma," Mama said. "Also, ants come in many different shapes and sizes, depending on what kind of life they live and what they eat. Did you know that an ant has two stomachs?"

"Wow! It would be great to have two stomachs, so I could eat as much as I wanted!" Chris exclaimed.

"Now, wait a minute!" Mama told him. "The ant was not created with two stomachs so that it could be greedy or selfish. Only one is for food for the ant itself. The other stomach is especially for sharing. The ant takes food back to its home to share with the other ants."

"Too bad," Chris sighed, pretending to be very disappointed.

Mama continued to tell Danielle and the older children about ants. "They have many different kinds of homes," she said. "Some dig tunnels in the ground. Others, like the big, red weaver ants, crawl up trees and 'glue' big leaves together to make their nest."

"You've seen the big nests out in the back yard," Emma reminded Danielle.

"I remember; in the mango tree," Danielle answered.

"Did you know that even the baby ants – the larvae – help to build those nests?" Mama asked. "The adults hold the larvae against the edges of the leaves, and a sticky, silky 'glue' comes out of the larvae and sticks the leaves together."

"Ants live together in big 'cities,' or 'colonies,'" Mama told the children. "There may be only ten or fifteen ants in some kinds of ant cities, but most colonies have a *lot*. Some have as many as 500,000 or even more ants living in them! With that many ants living together in one small place, they must not fight and argue like children sometimes do. Instead, they have to work together, always helping each other."

> *"Mommy, Mommy, come outside and look. Ebony's food is crawling up the wall!"*

A few days later, Danielle came running into the house, calling excitedly, "Mommy, Mommy, come outside and look. Ebony's food is crawling up the wall!"

Danielle liked to help feed the family's little black kitten, Ebony. Sometimes she would give it canned kitten food to eat. Other times she would put a few tiny pieces of dry cat food outside the door when Ebony meowed to say that she was hungry. Ebony would eat until her little tummy was full and fat. Sometimes, though, Danielle put out too much, and Ebony could not finish it all.

That is just what had happened this time, and now the left-over bits of dry cat food looked like they were crawling right up the wall! Higher and higher the pieces went until they reached the roof of the house. All around the chunks of kitty food were many, many ants, working together as hard as they could.

Mama watched what was going on, then she asked, "Danni, what would happen if all of those ants were selfish, and each one wanted the food for itself? How far up the wall would they get if each one started pulling the food toward itself?"

"Not very far. They might even fall down," Danielle answered.

"Right," Mama said. "But when they cooperate and work together, they can really surprise us. Remember the other day, when I told you that an ant has two stomachs; one for the ant's own food, and one for the rest of its very big family?"

"Yes, and Chris wished he had two stomachs so he could eat more!" Danielle laughed.

Mama smiled, then she began to tell Danielle a story. "When Worker Ant goes looking for food, other worker ants from its colony are also out hunting. When one finds food, it quickly shares the news with the others. Then all of the workers can go and eat until they are full.

"Some human boys and girls might be selfish, and they would want to keep it a secret so that they could have all the good food to themselves. Really, though, we should share when we find something nice, shouldn't we?"

Danielle nodded her head.

Mama continued, "Well, Worker Ant fills up with food, and then it goes home, where there are young ants and nurse ants that do not leave the colony. When Worker arrives, it may go to see them. Do you know what happens then? One of the stay-at-home ants uses the little antennae on its head and goes *tap, tap, tap* on Worker's abdomen." Mama tapped on Danielle's tummy, and she began to laugh and wiggle away. "Worker Ant quickly squeezes a drop of food out of its stomach so that the other ant can eat.

"One kind of ant, the honey ant, will even give its life for the other ants in its colony. At night, during the warm weather, these ants go out to a tree which has a special kind of honey called 'honeydew.' An ant fills its stomach with as much of the honeydew as it can hold, then it goes back home. But ants don't make honeycombs like bees do, so what should they do with all their honey?"

Danielle just shook her head, not sure what the worker ants should do.

So Mama told her, "Some give their whole lives to just help the others in their colony. They will offer to become storage tanks for the honeydew that comes back. They hang upside-down from the ceiling, waiting for a load of honey to come back to the colony.

"A storage tank ant drinks the honeydew from one carrier ant. Then from another. And another. Its stomach gets bigger and *bigger* and BIGGER! Its stomach gets eight or ten times as big as its normal size, until it looks like a balloon that is nearly ready to go *pop!*" Mama clapped her hands together loudly and Danielle jumped with surprise. Mama said, "It stores the honeydew until the cold weather, when there is no more in the trees. Then the ants of the colony can come and drink from it.

"A storage tank ant is so very full that it can not even move. If it ever fell off the ceiling where it hangs, its stomach really *would* burst, and it would die. Once a honey ant becomes a storage tank, it can never return to a normal life. It will be a storage tank until it dies, after spending its whole life working for the other ants in its colony."

Mama stopped talking for a few moments, then she said, "I've always tried to teach you children to share. When Chris was just a little boy and Emma was a tiny baby, he really loved her. He enjoyed helping me to take care of her. Whenever Chris shared a toy or something else nice, he would say to me, 'Look, Mommy, I'm a Share Brother!'"

Danielle giggled as she thought of Chris and Emma ever being so little.

"That's how we should be, too, isn't it?" Mama asked. "Just like the ants, we ought to be share brothers or share sisters, always trying to be helpful and to share what we have with others."

Look at the Ant

The Bible says, dear daughter or son,
Go look at the ant, you lazy one![1]
Get busy and help,
When there's work to be done.

---

[1] Prov. 6:6

No Entry: Camels Only

"Daddy, look at that sign!" Emma said excitedly. She pointed toward where a narrow dirt road turned off of the main highway. At its entrance, a sign read NO ENTRY for cars and trucks; the road was for camels only.

"What a funny sign," Chris exclaimed. "'Camels only'!"

Daddy was taking the family on a short vacation in northern Pakistan, and they were driving into an area where camels were common. Everyone enjoyed watching for the animals, which carried Afghan carpets and other heavy loads for many miles across the dry, hilly country.

"Did you know that in some parts of the world, camels are used instead of trucks to cross great, sandy deserts?" Daddy asked. "The camel has wide feet that won't sink into the sand. Those feet have tough padding so that the rocks on the rough mountain paths don't hurt them.

"Have you ever seen the one big hump on the back of an Arabian camel? Or the two humps on the Bactrian camel?" he continued. "Camels' humps are very important. They're not just for looks, and not for holding water like many people think, but for storing food, especially fat. A one-humped camel can store nearly 100 pounds of fat. That may be almost as much as Mama or Grandma Johnson weighs! That hump makes it possible for a camel to go across the desert or over the mountains without food or water for a week, even in the very hottest weather."

"Wow!" exclaimed Chris. "I'm sure glad Mom feeds us more than once every single day."

"I agree with that, Chris," Daddy answered. "Those camels may walk twenty-five miles or more each day. When a camel's body needs energy, it just uses some of the fat out of the hump. Camels also store quite a lot of water in their bodies, but they do not use it up quickly because they hardly sweat at all."

"Do you know what I read?" asked Mama. "In China, camels are used to carry food, mail, tools, and other supplies. In fact, at one bus stop in northern China, the road ends but passengers can still travel farther by buying tickets for a camel caravan, which will carry them onward to the villages in the desert. It's not a very comfortable trip, but at least it takes them there!

"As useful as the camel is, however," she continued, "it is *not* a very pleasant animal to be around. Camels often fight and bite each other. And whenever a load is put on its back, it groans about it."

"Does that remind you of anyone you know?" Daddy asked. "Sometimes boys and girls fuss and complain when they are asked to do something. If Mama needs help to carry something in from the car, have you ever heard anyone say, 'It's too heavy' or 'I'm too tired'? Or if you are playing a game or watching TV, and one of us asks you to do something, do you answer cheerfully and jump right up to help?"

"I remember something that happened when Chris and Emma were younger, and before Danielle was even born," Mama said. "Daddy was teaching at a boarding school in Pakistan then. Do you remember, Chris, when Uncle Quint and Auntie Norene came to visit us?" she asked.

Chris nodded.

"While they were with us, I wanted them to see what the village market was like," Mama told Emma and Danielle. "Usually I drove the car to the market, but I thought it would be more fun for Uncle and Auntie to go in one of those horse carts called a '*tonga*.'"

Chris spoke up. "You asked me to go out and watch for Taj when he came in his *tonga* to bring the vegetables to the cafeteria," he said, remembering the story well.

"Yes," continued Mama. "I told Chris, 'When Taj comes, tell him that we would like to go back to the market with him. Soon Chris came back, riding on the front seat of the *tonga* next to Taj, and ran into the house telling everyone to hurry because Taj was waiting."

"What's a '*tonga*,' Mommy?" asked Danielle.

"That's a cart for people to ride in, and it is pulled by a horse," answered Mama. "Lots of people there use them instead of cars." She then continued, "Well, Chris hadn't thought that the trip to the market would be anything special. He had been there many times, and usually he wanted to stay home … but since Auntie Norene and Uncle Quint were visiting, he decided to go along this time. Oh, what a trip it turned out to be!

"Uncle Quint and Auntie Norene enjoyed looking around at the village market," Mama remembered. "There were so many interesting things that they had never seen before. When we all finally got back into the *tonga* and started riding toward home, I asked Auntie Norene, 'Have you ever ridden on a camel?'"

Chris spoke up. "Auntie Norene looked really surprised. She answered, 'No, but that sounds like fun!'"

Mama continued, "So I turned and spoke to Taj in his language. Soon he turned the *tonga* around right in the middle of the road and went back into the village. We rode up one short street and started down another, and there, in the middle of one street, was a big, fuzzy, brown camel."

"Taj stopped and spoke to the camel driver," Chris continued the story. "Pretty soon he told Mama it was okay for them to take a ride. So everyone got down from the *tonga*, and the camel driver made the camel lie down. Then he pointed his stick at its back to show Auntie Norene where to get on. Even though it was lying down, she still had to *str-e-e-etch* hard to get her leg over the camel's back. Uncle Quint got on behind her, behind the camel's big hump."

Mama's eyes opened really wide as she looked at Danielle and said, "Just then everything seemed to go wrong! The camel began to roar – even louder than a lion, I think! It started to stand up – but a camel doesn't just stand straight up. It rocks forward and backward, like a little boat on giant ocean waves. As this camel rocked, Uncle Quint slid right off the back!"

Chris added, "That left Auntie Norene up on the camel all by herself, while Uncle Quint and I stood there watching. Mama just started snapping pictures with her camera. That old camel kept roaring as it started racing down the street. The driver was holding onto the rope as tightly as possible, but that awful camel was almost dragging him … and poor Auntie Norene was really, really scared!"

Mama spoke up, "At last the driver got the camel to stop running and lie down. Auntie Norene was so afraid that she was shaking all over, and she was almost crying. But that old camel was still snorting, showing its teeth, and complaining about its work!"

As Mama finished telling the story, Chris and Emma were laughing, while Danielle still looked a bit worried about poor Auntie Norene, up there on the camel all by herself!

"Complaining and grumbling don't sound nice coming from a camel," Daddy said, "but they sound even worse coming from a boy or a girl. It's good to work cheerfully. Even when the teacher assigns too much homework, or your mother asks you to do some chores, keep smiling!"

"Do you remember, Chris and Emma, when you were a bit younger," Mama asked, "how sometimes, when we were working in the garden, one of you would get tired and start to fuss?"

"I do," Emma answered. "I remember that little song we used to sing. Whenever one of us would start to complain, you would start humming or whistling our little work song."

Mama began to whistle, and soon both Chris and Emma were singing along with her: "You can whistle while you work, hum-hum-hum-hum-hum-hum-hum. You can whistle while you work. Then the work you have won't seem so bad, if you whistle while you work." Even Daddy and Danielle had joined in before they finished.

After they were done singing, Daddy said, "What I remember is that whenever you sang that song, in just a little while, *everyone* was singing or whistling. And sure enough, the work wasn't so bad after all."

The Grumbler

The great humpy camel
Is as strong as can be,
Called "The ship of the desert"
Crossing the wide, sandy "sea."
With loads big and heavy
High up on his back,
Taking carpets or people
Or a large mail sack,
He can walk for days
Without water or food,
But nothing compares
With a camel's bad mood!
With other camels
He's likely to fight;
When the master loads him,
He may try to bite.
Oh, don't be like a camel
That fusses and roars
When Mom or Dad asks you
To help with the chores.
Be joyful, be happy,
Be a helpful daughter or son.
Keep smiling, be cheerful
When there's work to be done.

Starfish and Broken Arms

Chris, Emma and Danielle loved to go to the beach. Sometimes, for a special vacation, Daddy would take the whole family to some of the nice ones in Thailand. They especially liked swimming among the colorful fish and coral along one beautiful beach near Phuket. There were some pretty sea shells on another of their favorite beaches. On yet another beach nearby, there was something even more special.

There, holding on to some big rocks, were lots and lots of bright, orange-colored starfish. Many of the starfish they saw were bigger than Daddy's hand. All of them had five long arms and looked like pretty, five-pointed stars. For a long time, the children thought all starfish looked just like that.

Then one December they saw a starfish that did not have long arms. In fact, while it did have five points like a star, it had no arms at all. It was fat like a sponge, and it felt like rubber.

Daddy held the starfish on his hand for a few minutes as they walked down the beach. Soon Danielle asked, "May I hold it, Daddy?"

Imagine everybody's surprise when Daddy turned the starfish upside down into Danielle's hand and found his handprint on the bottom of the starfish! Then everyone wanted to hold it and see their own handprints on it.

After they had all had a chance to carry it, Daddy said, "Let me carry it again for a while, Emma. It probably isn't good to handle it too much." Daddy took off one of his large sandals and held it out with the bottom facing up, and Emma placed the starfish on it.

In a few minutes, Daddy turned the starfish over once again, curious to find out what it looked like now. Sure enough: there, on the bottom of the starfish, were the same wiggly lines as the tread of his sandals.

A few months later, the children went to a big aquarium. There they were surprised to see several other kinds of starfish that were different shapes and sizes. They were even more surprised when they found out that there were about 2,000 different types in the world!

What's more, they learned, starfish didn't all have five arms. Most did, but one kind had six. Some had ten. There were even kinds with twenty, thirty, forty, or even *fifty* arms!

"Oh, my, what would you do with fifty arms?" Daddy teased. "Wouldn't you be afraid that they might get all tangled up?"

On another day, while Mama was out shopping, her friend Meggi came to babysit Danielle. Auntie Meggi was usually very cheerful, but not that day. Even little Danielle was sure that something was wrong. After a while, she asked, "Auntie Meggi, why are you so sad?"

"I just got a letter from my mother," Auntie Meggi answered. "Last week she fell down and broke her arm. Now it hurts so much that it is hard for her to work."

"Oh, no!" Poor little Danielle almost cried at the news.

Auntie Meggi was usually very cheerful, but not that day. Even little Danielle was sure that something was wrong.

After a while, Mama came home and Auntie Meggi left. "Mommy, Mommy," Danielle said excitedly, "do you know what happened to Auntie Meggi's mommy?"

"No, what happened, Danni?" Mama asked.

"Oh, Mommy," she said with a worried look on her face, "Auntie Meggi's mommy fell and broke her arm." For a few moments, Danielle was quiet.

Then she asked, "Mommy, will the doctor be able to put Auntie Meggi's mommy's arm back on again?"

Mommy smiled. *Now* she knew why Danielle was so worried. "Oh, Danni," Mama said gently, "her mommy's arm did not fall off. Inside of the skin, her bone got cracked when she fell, but it will get better. The doctors just put a nice, white plaster cast on her arm to hold it very, very still. If the bone cannot wiggle around, then it will slowly begin to grow back together. After a few weeks it should be all okay again."

Danielle looked very relieved.

Then Mama told her something that she had read. "Sometimes starfish lose one of their arms. They might even lose two or three. Maybe a crab pinches one off, or maybe a fish bites it off, or something else happens to it. Even though that is sad, it doesn't matter too much, because even if a starfish loses all but one of its arms, it is still all right. Do you know why?"

Danielle shook her head.

"Because a starfish can grow new arms," Mama told her.

"Really?" Danielle asked, very surprised.

Mama began to tell a story. "One time a group of fishermen got very angry at all the starfish. These fishermen worked every day, getting oysters and abalone to bring back to sell at the fish market. The trouble was that starfish like to eat abalone, oysters, crabs, and clams, too, so they were spoiling the fishermen's business.

"The fishermen thought and thought about what to do. Finally they decided to pay some men with boats to go and catch as many starfish as they could. So the boat men went out and started working. They caught hundreds and hundreds of them.

"Then the fishermen told them, 'Now cut all the starfish in half, and throw them back into the water.'"

Danielle made an awful face and said, "But Mommy, that's so mean!"

"Yes, it is," Mama said. Then she went on, "Those fishermen thought that they would kill the starfish by cutting them up. They didn't know that if some of the middle part of a starfish is left with even one arm, it will grow into a new starfish. So when the men cut them in half, what do you think happened?"

"I don't know," Danielle answered, looking very worried.

"Almost every piece that they threw back into the water grew into a new starfish," Mama told her. "Then those fishermen really did have a big problem. They had twice as many starfish eating their oysters and abalone as they'd had before! They should not have been unkind to such pretty animals. It's good to protect and take care of the beautiful things in nature, isn't it?"

Danielle nodded.

"Yet even though those starfish had something very bad happen to them, they didn't give up. They are *persistent*; they just keep on trying."

"They're what?" Danielle asked.

"Per-*sis*-tent," Mama repeated. "Even when it is eating, a starfish is persistent. A hungry one will let go of the rock it is holding on to and let the water carry it along until it finds something good to eat." Then Mama asked, "Do you remember how sometimes we use little hooks or baskets in the shower, that just stick on by a circle of rubber on the back?"

"Yes," answered Danielle.

"Most of those stick because they have some little suction cups on them. Well, the bottom of a starfish has hundreds and hundreds of tiny little suction cups. They are very strong. If you try to pull a starfish away from the rock where it is resting, it will be really hard to get it loose.

"And if it finds a nice clam to eat, the starfish uses these hundreds of little suction cups to hold on to the two sides of the clam shell. Then it slowly pulls, trying to open up the clam so that it can eat the inside. It just keeps pulling and pulling and never gives up."

"Like when Daddy plays tug-of-war with Chris and Emma and me?" asked Danielle.

"Yes, sort of like that," Mama answered. "After a long time, the clam gets tired, just like you do in tug-of-war, and it stops even trying to stay closed. When the clam's shell opens wide enough, the stomach of the starfish comes right out of its mouth."

"Ooh, yuck!" Danielle made an awful face.

Mama laughed, then she said, "That stomach turns inside out and moves into the clam's shell. There the stomach begins to eat up the meat of the clam. When the starfish has finished, it pulls its stomach back inside its body, then it lets go of the shell and floats happily on its way."

Danielle giggled.

"What would happen if the starfish gave up pulling before it got the clam shell open?" Mama asked.

"He would still be hungry," answered Danielle.

"He certainly would!" Mama answered. "Have you ever heard a boy or girl say, 'I can't do it'? Or maybe you've heard someone say, 'It's too hard for me', 'That song is too difficult for me to play', 'I can't do this homework!', or 'I just can't learn how to do this.' Sometimes children – or even big people – just want to give up when something is not as easy as they would like.

"If they just quit, they cannot hope to succeed, can they? But if they keep trying and working and trying some more, they will usually be able to do it at last. Now, do you remember that big word I taught you a few minutes ago?" Mama asked Danielle.

"Pers … I forgot," said Danielle.

"It's a big word," Mama told her, "but that word 'persistence' is a very good one to know and a very important habit to have. When you are trying to do something good, even if it is very difficult, keep trying. Don't give up until you finish it. Be just like the starfish, that is so persistent that it won't let anything stop it. Never give up; never quit until you have finished."

Keep Trying

Don't give up
If there's some work you have to do.
Don't cry, don't sigh – just try!
Don't give up 'till the work is through.

Adapa-what?

Emma happened to be outside, and she heard her neighbor across the fence talking. "Mommy, what are we having for dinner tonight?" asked six-year-old Kathy. Emma couldn't quite hear what Kathy's mother answered, but she did hear a grumbling little voice answer, "But Mom, I don't like that! I don't want that for dinner."

Imagine Emma's surprise when she heard the answer Kathy's mother gave: "I'm sorry, Kathy, that's all this restaurant is serving tonight!"

Kathy continued to whine and complain, while Emma, who thought it was such a funny answer, began to giggle. She hurried inside to tell Mama, and together they both laughed.

"I'm really thankful that you and Chris don't complain about your food," Mama told Emma. "You two children are really easy to cook for, and I appreciate that. Usually Danielle eats everything too, although once in a while she makes a little fuss."

"Why do other kids complain so much, Mom?" Emma wondered aloud. "Ryan and Robert are always saying 'I don't like this' or 'I don't like that.' They never like anything their mom cooks! And when they come here to eat, they won't ever try anything new. They just ask, 'What's this?' and won't even take one bite."

"I know, Emma. Auntie Julia must have a very hard time cooking for them. Remember, though, that Uncle Jacob dislikes many kinds of food, too. I'm afraid that the boys have learned it from their father. He doesn't want to taste anything new or different, either."

"I think you're lucky, Mom," Emma answered. "Daddy likes your cooking, and so do I!"

Mama patted Emma on the shoulder. "I am lucky, for sure. Do you know what my family reminds me of?"

"No, what?" Emma wanted to know.

"The sparrows."

Emma wondered why Mama would say that they were like sparrows.

"You wait until dinnertime," Mama answered, "when Chris and Danni are here too. Then I'll tell all of you."

Emma was curious, but Mama would not tell her any more just then.

When everyone was sitting at the table and eating that evening, Emma said, "Mom, you promised to tell us tonight: why are Chris and Danni and I like the sparrows?"

"Because you are adaptable," Mama answered.

"Adapa-what?" Chris joked.

Mama laughed. "A-*dapt*-a-ble," she repeated.

"What does that mean, Mommy?" little Danielle asked.

"Well, first let me tell you about the sparrows. Do you know what they eat?" Mama looked at each of the children to see if they had any ideas.

"Worms?" Danielle guessed first.

"Seeds," Chris stated, sounding very sure of himself.

Emma shook her head, not sure what else to answer. "Seeds, I guess … or do they eat flies and other insects?"

"Good, you're all correct!" Mama said. Then she went on to tell the children more about the little birds that they saw around their house every day. "Sparrows are very adaptable. That means, for example, that they aren't picky about what they eat. They don't complain about where they have to live, either. People have taken sparrows to many, many parts of the world, and they can live almost anywhere, in hot or cold weather.

"Mom, you promised to tell us tonight: why are Chris and Danni and I like the sparrows?"

Mama continued, "When families go on vacation to new places, sometimes the children complain about the different kinds of food, but sparrows just eat whatever they find, wherever they go. If they could always choose, they would like to eat seeds; especially rice, wheat, or other grains. But if they can't find those, they will eat something else.

"Sparrows are happy to eat fruit, for example. And sometimes you might see them picking dead moths or insects off of a car or a truck, or catching the bugs that fly around outdoor lights. They will eat earthworms, snails, or small frogs. And if they cannot find anything else, they will even eat the meat of dead animals."

"Ooh, that is *yuck*!" Emma said, making a terrible face.

Mama laughed, then went on to say, "If you throw a bit of rice or other food out on the grass or driveway, what do you think will happen a few minutes later? If you stay back so that you don't scare them, you will probably see some sparrows and other birds coming to enjoy your food!"

"Remember," Daddy said, "how Mama told us that sparrows live almost anywhere? Most of us like to have our own place to stay, with comfortable rooms and our own beds, but the little sparrows seem happy wherever they live, whether it is in a tree out in the countryside or in a large warehouse in the middle of a big city. They can build their nests almost anywhere and still they keep singing their chirpy little songs."

Mama began to tell a story. "Once, when Emma was just a baby and Chris was a little boy, there were two little sparrows that thought they had found a perfect place to build a nest. Chris watched them every day."

"Where was that?" Chris wanted to know.

"When your dad was teaching at the boarding school, you liked to go to his office so you could walk home with him for lunch and dinner," Mama answered Chris. "The small air conditioner in the wall of his office dripped water onto the sidewalk by the auditorium, so he hung an empty paint bucket under it to catch the drips."

"That must have looked funny!" giggled Danielle.

"Well, the sparrows didn't think it looked funny," Mama said, smiling. "In fact, they thought it looked like a very nice place for a nest. Soon they started to bring pieces of dry grass. Both the mother and father worked together to build it.

"But Daddy didn't want the sparrows to make a nest in the paint bucket, so every second or third day he would pull out all the grass."

"Daddy, that was mean!" Emma scolded him.

"I wasn't trying to be unkind to them, Emma," Daddy told her. "I only knew that if they built a nest there, it would soon be spoiled by the dripping water. I just wanted to encourage them to build their nest in a safer place."

"Those two sparrows were certainly *persistent* little creatures," Mama said. "Remember that word which we learned the other day? Those two birds just kept on trying and would not give up."

"Whatever happened to them?" Chris asked.

"Hmm," Mama said, "I'm not really sure. Maybe your dad can remember."

Then Chris looked at Daddy for an answer.

"Well," Daddy said, "I don't know how the story finally ended. As long as I was teaching at that school, those two little sparrows never did give up trying to build a nest in that paint bucket!" He thought a moment, then continued, "And actually, those weren't the only sparrows that were 'adaptable,' to use Mama's big new word.

"The auditorium across from my office had very large windows with no screens on them. Sparrows used to fly in and out all day long. Even during school assembly time, they would fly around and chirp. They tried to build their nests everywhere: above the windows, on the stage curtains, and even on top of the ceiling fans!"

Chris, Emma and Danielle all looked up at the fan above them and tried to imagine a bird building a nest there. "That's adaptable!" Chris exclaimed.

"That's right," Mama answered. "That's being happy wherever you are, and with whatever you have. You'll still be happy, even if – like Kathy's mother said – 'that's all this restaurant is serving tonight!'"

Stay Happy

Whatever the weather, be it sunny or gray,
Keep smiling, stay happy, be cheerful anyway.
Wherever you live, however the place,
Just make it your home: keep a smile on your face!
Whatever you're eating, however the food,
Eat it with joy; keep a bright, happy mood.
Whatever may happen, whatever goes wrong,
Just be like the sparrow … keep singing a song.

Oh, Rats!

"Auntie Sydney phoned me a while ago," Mama told the children after dinner. "She had a rat in her garage again today!"

Emma looked unhappy and said, "Oh, *gross!*"

"I'm afraid so. This is the second time, and her sweet dog Trixie doesn't even seem to care. Uncle David was finally able to trap it when he got home from work this evening."

"Boy, I'm sure glad for that!" Emma exclaimed.

Daddy was listening and spoke up, "Rats seem to be able to live almost anywhere. And I've read about how hard it is to get rid of them. After a volcano erupts, for example, the rats may be some of the first animals to come back to that area. I also once learned that they could fall off of a four- or five-story building, land on their feet, and still live!"

"Wow!" Chris said, looking very surprised.

"Wait 'till you hear this, though," Daddy continued. "They can hold their breath for quite a few minutes, which means you could flush a rat down the toilet, and it could live through it!"

"You're joking, aren't you?" Emma asked him.

"Not at all," Daddy said. "In fact, they can climb up a drain pipe into a toilet bowl and get *into* your house that way!"

"Oh, that's yucky!" Danielle wrinkled up her nose at the thought of a rat being in the toilet then running around the house with its dirty feet.

> *Daddy knows all about rats and drain pipes. We have a real story to tell about that.*

"Daddy knows all about rats and drain pipes," Mama started talking now. "We have a real story to tell about that," she said, laughing. "This happened when Chris was just a baby, and we were living in Pakistan.

"One evening we were getting ready to go to a meeting at the church. I was dressed and ready to go, but Daddy still needed to take his shower. He started taking off his clothes, and all of a sudden this big ugly rat jumped right up onto his bare leg! Daddy jumped in the air and let out a loud yell. Then he slammed the bathroom door shut so the rat couldn't get out."

"I thought at the time that it couldn't get out with the door closed," Daddy said, "but maybe it could have. I have learned since then that rats can get through very small holes and other tight spaces. I once watched a mouse squeeze right under a door where there was almost no room at all to get through."

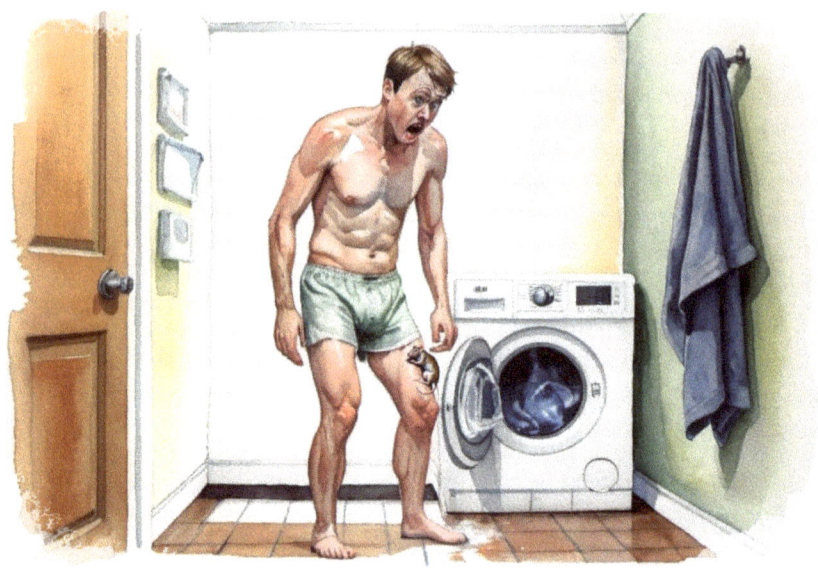

"And they can chew right through wood and other hard things, too," Mama added. "Actually, that helps to keep their teeth from getting too long. Somewhere I read that a rat's teeth grow four or five inches in a year!"

"Really?" Danielle exclaimed.

"Really, truly," Mama answered. "Anyway, let me tell you the rest of the story about Daddy's rat. Daddy called to me and asked me to bring the *dahnda*; a long, round piece of wood that we used for grinding up spices. It sort of looked like a small baseball bat without the handle. I took it into the bathroom, shutting the door very quickly behind me to try to keep the rat inside.

"I handed the *dahnda* to Daddy, but the rat had run and hidden under the little washing machine in the bathroom. Daddy banged and banged that wooden stick against the front of the washer, but the rat would not come back out."

"I still needed to get ready to go to the meeting at church," said Daddy, "so I quickly took my shower. I rubbed and scrubbed my leg where the rat had landed, and you can be sure I used a lot of soap! I also had Mama put some strong medicine all over that part of my leg so it wouldn't get infected. Then I got dressed to go to the meeting."

Mama interrupted and asked, "Do you know why Daddy was so worried about scrubbing his leg so well and putting so much medicine on it?"

Chris answered. "Rats carry all kinds of diseases."

"Like typhus! I saw that in old movies on TV," said Emma. She added, "Anne Frank and her sister died from typhus."

"That's right, Chris and Emma," Mama said. "Probably the worst disease ever was something that was carried by fleas riding along on rats. It was the bubonic plague, also called the 'Black Death.' That was about 700 years ago. It spread through many of the countries of northern Africa, Europe, and Asia. That plague lasted for quite a few years, and they think that at least 800 people died from it every day! That meant that millions and millions of people died from it in total."

Danielle looked like she was about to start crying, and Mama told her, "We don't have to worry about the bubonic plague now, Danni. There are some very good medicines to prevent it and treat it."

"So, what happened with Daddy's rat?" Emma wanted to know.

"Well," Mama answered, "before we left the house, we found all the ant and other insect spray that I had in the house. Daddy opened the door to the bathroom just enough so that he could spray and spray and spray, until he had emptied every can!"

"Did it kill the rat?" Chris asked.

"I didn't know," Daddy answered, "but we went to our meeting, wondering what we would find when we got home."

Really curious now, Emma asked, "So what *did* you find?"

Daddy told her, "First you should know that in the shower, covering the opening of the drain pipe, was a round piece of metal that was about four or five inches across. It had quite a few holes in it for the water to run through. But that cover wasn't hooked onto anything, so even before I started spraying, I had put a small empty bucket over the whole drain.

"Now, when we got home, we went right into the bathroom to see what had happened with our rat," Daddy continued. "What we found was a real surprise.

"It seemed like that old rat had pushed the bucket away. Then he must have clawed at the metal drain cover until he got it off. The cover was pushed an inch or two away, just sitting on the floor of the shower; and there was the drain hole, completely open. Our awful rat was gone!"

"Wow! That's cool!" Chris exclaimed.

"Is there anything we can learn from the rat?" Mama asked all three children.

"They're bad!" Danielle was the first to speak.

"They're everywhere, causing trouble," Emma added.

"Does that remind you of anyone?" Mama asked.

"Satan?" Emma answered.

"That's right," Daddy said. "Did I invite that rat into our house?" he asked.

"No way!" Chris said.

"I certainly didn't! But it came in anyway, just like Satan does. We don't need to invite him to come into our lives; he will find a way to get in. Then he will try to make trouble. He would like to make us sick. He wants to make us do bad things, or make us not believe in God."

Mama had a thought, too. "The rat seems to be able to eat bait that is put out for it without getting caught, and it seems like it can get out of almost any kind of trap if it *does* get caught. That's what Auntie Sydney's rat kept doing. Rats are very smart and clever.

"Satan is also very clever," Mama continued. "He knows us so well that he knows how he might tempt us to do wrong. He wants to ruin our lives. But the Bible tells us in James chapter four, verses seven and eight, that we need to do what God wants us to do. It says to 'resist the devil,' to run away from him! And 'give yourselves to God. Stand against the devil, and he will run away from you. Come near to God and He will come near to you.[2]'"

"That's right," Daddy said. "So how can we 'come near to God?'"

"By reading the Bible," Emma was the first to answer.

"Right, Emma. Jesus did that, and He is our example. His mother had taught him Bible verses from the time he was very little. And then He studied the Bible messages for Himself so that He knew the Bible very, very well. That helped him to obey God when Satan tempted Him.

Daddy continued, "Satan will try to make sin look really good or fun. But if we know what the Bible teaches, we can say, like Jesus did, 'It is written…'"

"But Satan knows the Bible too!" Chris said.

"That's true, Chris," Daddy answered. "But he will use it in a wrong way to try to make us sin. That's why we need to know the Bible very well. We should be like King David when he said, 'I have hidden Your word in my heart so that I won't sin against You[3].' That's how we can keep that bad rat, Satan, from making us sick with sin!"

---

[2] ERV.
[3] NIRV.

Dirty Helpers

Mama and the two girls came home from the nursery one day with three plants in flowerpots. Two were rose bushes and looked as if they would soon have dozens of brightly-colored flowers on them. Emma thought that they would look very pretty alongside the driveway. The other pot had a nice gardenia plant with sweet-smelling white flowers.

Danielle put her nose up close to one blossom. She sniffed its sweet perfume. "Mmm, I like this one!" she said.

"Emma," called Mama, "please go call Daddy and Chris to help us dig the holes so we can plant these in the ground."

Soon Daddy and Chris came out of the house. "Where do you want them?" Daddy asked.

Emma rushed to show him where she and Mama had decided to put the roses. Then Mama pointed out where to plant the gardenia. While Daddy carried the heavy pots to the right places, Chris hurried to find a shovel.

When he came back, he started to dig a hole where they would plant the pretty gardenia. After a while Chris got tired, so Daddy took his turn digging. More and more soil came out of the hole, until Daddy stopped digging for a moment to wipe the sweat from his face.

Suddenly Danielle noticed part of a little pink worm sticking out of the side of the hole. "Look, Daddy!" she called with delight. She knelt down on the ground and reached for the worm. Gently she began to pull, but the worm did not come out of the dirt. She pulled a little more, but the worm just seemed to *s-t-r-e-t-c-h*. "Can you get it out for me, Daddy. Please?" she asked.

Carefully, Daddy dug a little more dirt away, and the worm fell into the bottom of the hole. Danielle quickly reached down, picked it up, and held it in her hand. The worm started to wiggle.

"*Ooh*, it feels funny!" she giggled. "Find some more, Daddy," she begged. Daddy began digging again, but suddenly Danielle started crying so loudly that Mama and Emma both came running to see what was the matter.

Danielle pointed into the hole and cried, "Daddy, you cut that poor little worm in half. Now he's going to die!" Then she cried some more.

Mama put her arms around Danielle to comfort her. "You know, Danni, you really don't need to worry about the little worm dying. Do you know why?"

Danielle shook her head.

"Because if an earthworm gets cut in half, it can usually grow a new front or back," Mama told her. "Later you might see only a little scar where the worm got cut but grew again.

She continued, "Do you see all these tiny rings around the worm? Each ring is called a 'segment,' and an adult earthworm may have about 200 of these segments. Unless, of course, you go to Australia, where you will find earthworms that are nine or ten feet long or more!"

"Wow! That long?" exclaimed Emma.

"Danni, remember how it felt when you tried to pull that earthworm out of the ground?" Daddy asked.

Danielle nodded. "Yes: he was stuck."

"He seemed to be," Daddy answered. "Actually, he was just holding on tightly."

"But, Daddy, an earthworm doesn't have any hands," Danielle said.

"True," Daddy told her, "but the worm does have bristles, which are like stiff hairs or little hooks that he can stick out when he needs them. Almost every one of those segments has eight tiny bristles, which we may not even see, and they are pointed toward the back of the worm so that if you try to pull, he can just dig into the soil and hold on tightly. That can really help the worm when a bird digs down and grabs hold of him!"

"It's like the bird and the worm are playing tug-of-war," Chris said.

"Daddy, why did the worm stretch so much when I pulled him?" Danielle wanted to know.

"Well, Danni, an earthworm constantly stretches and shrinks, whether it is down in the ground or on top of it. That's how it moves," said Daddy. "First your worm uses one set of muscles to stretch the front of his body out ahead of him: that's how he goes forward. Then he uses the other set of muscles to pull his back end toward the front, which makes him short and fat. As the worm stretches and shrinks, he slowly travels. All those bristles also help him to keep going forward without slipping back."

Danielle looked closely at the worm in her hand, trying to see any bristles. Then Chris spoke up, warning her, "You'd better put that earthworm back in the ground before he dies!"

"I'm not hurting him," she argued.

"If he dries out, he will die," Chris answered.

"No he won't, will he, Mommy?" Danielle looked at Mama, hoping that her mother would agree with her.

"I'm afraid that Chris is right, Danielle," Mama said. "An earthworm is usually okay with a lot of water, but it can easily die if it gets too dry. That's why earthworms can live where it rains a lot but not in deserts."

"Remember where we used to live?" Chris said. "When it rained really hard for a long time, we would see hundreds of earthworms in the puddles on the dirt roadway."

Danielle looked worried. "Didn't they drown?" she asked.

"No," Mama answered. "Their tunnels got full of water, so they came up to the surface. Then, after the water was gone, most of the worms crawled back underground."

After a few moments, Chris looked at his little sister and asked, "Hey, Danni, do you know what your little earthworms eat?"

"No, what?"

Sometimes – like now – Chris enjoyed teasing his two sisters. He waited eagerly to see what Danielle's face would look like when he told her the answer. "Dirt," he said.

Danielle wrinkled up her face and said in disbelief, "Dirt? No! You're just teasing me again." She turned to Daddy and asked, "They don't really, do they, Daddy?"

"Well, Danni," Daddy answered, "Chris is partly correct. They do eat soil sometimes. If the ground is nice and soft, they normally just push their way through it. However, if the ground is very hard, they *eat* their way through."

"Oh, yucky!" Danielle groaned.

Daddy continued, "Sometimes earthworms eat soil that has little bits of rotten plants in it. They also sometimes eat the bodies of insects and other tiny animals. But usually they eat dead leaves and sticks. Earthworms often pull leaves down into their tunnels and eat them later."

"That doesn't sound very yummy!" said Emma.

"No, it doesn't sound good to us, but earthworms are made to help clean up dead plants. Did you know that earthworms are probably the best friends a gardener or farmer has?" asked Daddy.

"Really?" Danielle asked in surprise. "Why?"

Mama answered, "One reason is that their tunnels loosen the soil; then plant roots can grow through the ground more easily. Also, rainwater soaks into the ground better, instead of just running off and going to waste. Plus, as the worm eats, the waste that comes out its other end is very good fertilizer. It is full of good things which help plants to grow."

"Did you children know," asked Daddy, "that in a field of good farmland about the size of a football field, there may be two million earthworms or even more? Sometimes farmers use tractors to plow their land and make the soil looser, and if they are lucky, they may have millions of tiny little worms 'plowing' all the time!"

Mama added, "I heard of an interesting experiment you can do. Take two flowerpots and put some earthworms in the soil in one of them. Make sure that there are no earthworms in the *other* pot. Then plant the same kind of flowers or plants in each pot. They say that the plants in the pot with the earthworms will grow much bigger."

"Really? The earthworms don't do anything bad?" Danielle wanted to know.

Mama shook her head. "I don't think so."

"I have never heard of anything harmful either, Danni," Daddy answered. "Earthworms are probably some of the most helpful animals in the world. They are always at work helping and serving us.

"I think we could learn a good lesson from them, couldn't we? An earthworm spends its whole life serving and helping others, always being useful. That's how we should be too, isn't it?"

"I remember when Chris was just two or three years old," Mama said. "While he helped me to take care of baby Emma or to put away his toys, he used to sing. One of his favorite songs was, 'I'm a Happy, Happy Helper.' He would sing it over and over. I hope all three of you children will always be useful and helpful in every way possible."

"You know," Daddy said, "that makes me think of something very important in the Bible. There is a story in the book of Matthew, chapter twenty-five, that tells about how Jesus decides who should go to heaven and who should not. Here's what He says:

"'I was hungry and you gave me something to eat. I was thirsty, and you gave me a drink. I needed clothes, and you gave me something to wear. I was sick, and you took care of me.'[4]

"Then Jesus said that if we do those things for one of the people He made, it is like we are doing it for Him; and that it will be the 'happy, happy helpers' who get to go with Him to heaven."

Happy Helpers

The little earthworms in the ground
Are as busy as can be,
Though often we don't notice them
When they're down where we can't see.
They stretch and shrink as they move along
Above or beneath the ground,
So sometimes they look long and thin
And sometimes short and round.
If somehow they get cut in two,
They never seem to mind:
They simply grow another part
In front or else behind.
Those little earthworms help us all
By digging up the soil.
They do their job without complaint
About their work and toil.
So whether you are young or old,

---

[4] GW.

Or if you're short or tall,
It doesn't matter who you are
Or where you live, and all:
There's still some help that you can give,
Something useful you can do.
By helping others you will find
That you'll be happy too.

The Deadly Beauty

Going to Uncle Roger and Auntie Rosie's house was special for everyone in the family. Often the children felt very bored when they had to go to visit Mama and Daddy's friends, but they never felt that way at Uncle Roger and Auntie Rosie's home. Auntie's food was always delicious, and the table looked so pretty every time they went. That wasn't all that made it special, though.

Uncle Roger had been collecting sea shells for many years. He had found them all around the world in places where he worked or went on vacation. He had a wonderful display of the most beautiful ones. What's more, Uncle Roger always had many interesting stories to tell about his shells.

One Sunday while they were visiting, Danielle was looking at the lovely collection. "Uncle Roger, tell us another story about your sea shells. Please?"

Uncle Roger got up from his chair and walked toward the glass shelves where Danielle was standing. "Let me see, what shall I tell you about today?" He rubbed his chin as he thought.

"How about one of those cone shell stories that you shared with me the other day?" Daddy suggested. "The children haven't heard those."

"Okay," Uncle Roger agreed. Then he told the children, "Look over here: these are some of the cones I've found. There are more than 500 different kinds, so I still have many more to discover!"

"Wow, these are nice!" Emma exclaimed as she looked at textile cones and others with unusual patterns. "They look like someone painted all kinds of pretty designs on them."

"Did you know that cones are just snails that live in the ocean?" asked Uncle Roger.

"Really?" asked Danielle.

"It's true," Uncle Roger assured her. "Most of them live in warm, tropical oceans, around coral or just in the sand. You can find them moving around on top of the coral at night, which is why a lot of shell collectors go out at that time." He stopped talking for a minute while he picked out three or four cones and showed them to the children. "You can also find them in the daytime, though. Often I have gone out with a little shovel to dig in the sand around the coral, where they hide during the day. One day I found eight different kinds."

"May I hold this one?" Danielle asked.

"Yes, you may," Uncle Roger told her, "but don't ever, *ever* pick up a live cone at the beach, Danni. Do you see this small opening at the narrow end of the cone?"

Danielle nodded.

"That is where the snail puts out its long pink nose, called a 'proboscis,' which looks like a worm with a sharp tooth on the end of it." Uncle Roger continued, "The cone uses the proboscis like a dart or spear to shoot poison into a passing fish, worm, or other small animal it wants to eat. Even people can get stung, though, when they carelessly pick up a cone shell."

"Oh … does it hurt bad?" Danielle asked with a worried look on her face.

"With some types," Uncle Roger answered, "it is very painful. With many, it really doesn't hurt much more than a bee sting. But that sting can be very dangerous! Many people have died from cone shell stings."

Danielle's eyes opened wide with surprise. "Really?" she asked.

"Yes, Danni. When I was living in Guam, I knew an old man whose son, Samuel, died after picking up a cone shell."

Uncle Roger began his story. "Samuel was about thirty years old, and one day he went out fishing with his friends. They liked to fish around the coral reef on Kosrae Island. That reef had a lot of beautiful sea shells, too. It was low tide, and Samuel saw a very nice *Conus geographus* that was about three inches long."

"*Conus* what?" asked Chris.

"A *Conus geographus*: a geography cone shell."

"A 'geography cone!'" Chris and the girls laughed. "That's a funny name. Why is it called that?"

"I'm not too sure," Uncle Roger answered. "Maybe because its dark, irregular, purplish-brown patches look like a map of the world."

Emma looked at the cone shell, then said, "It looks like the pictures of the earth that they take from way out in space."

Uncle Roger smiled and nodded his head, then he continued. "Anyway, Samuel saw this nice geography cone, and he leaned down to pick it up. He put it into the pocket of his cut-off blue jeans and went on fishing."

"Oh, no!" Danielle gasped. She looked afraid to hear the rest.

"After a while," Uncle Roger said, "that cone shell stung Samuel right through his pants. He may not have felt it right away: sometimes the pain comes later. But when he realized that he had been stung, he quickly reached into his pocket and pulled out the cone.

"Now, geography cone shells are different from other cones. Most just have a narrow, open area along the side, but the geography cone has a very wide opening: the snail inside can stretch much of its body right outside of the shell if it wants to."

Chris, Emma and Danielle all watched Uncle Roger anxiously, waiting to hear what would happen next.

"Well, suddenly the shell stung Samuel again. He knew that he was in real trouble, so he quickly started wading to the shore. When he got to the beach, he fell down onto the sand. His friends ran to carry him to get help, but it was too late."

Chris and Emma were both very quiet for a while. Little Danielle looked as if she was about to cry. Finally Emma spoke up, "The cones look so pretty. How can they be like that?"

Daddy slowly began to speak. "Emma, people have told you and Danielle that you are pretty. Do you remember what Mama sometimes reminds you? She says that beauty is only skin deep."

"I know," Emma said, "or 'pretty is as pretty does.' I don't like it when she says that!"

"I know," Daddy looked at Emma, "but a person is only pretty if he or she *acts* pretty, right?"

As Mama helped to bring the food out to the table, she heard this part of the conversation. She said, "One of the teachers I used to work with, Diane, had so many bumps and pockmarks that she didn't *look* pretty at all. She always felt ugly and unhappy about the way she looked.

Mama paused. "Then one day during school assembly we heard one of the other teachers talk about inner beauty; being beautiful in one's words and actions. Diane listened very carefully, and at the end she leaned close to me and said quietly, 'You know, I was planning to get surgery to try to make my face look nicer. Now I know that isn't really important. I just need to work on having a beautiful character and being a nice person inside.'"

"That reminds me of a really good Bible verse," said Daddy. "First Samuel, chapter sixteen, verse seven. It says that we look at the outside of a person, like their face and hair and clothes, or maybe their house, or the car their mom and dad drive. But God looks at our hearts."

"Can you think of some things that make a person ugly inside?" asked Uncle Roger.

"Being mean or unkind," Chris suggested.

"Getting angry all the time," Emma said, "or being bossy."

Danielle thought for a moment, then said, "Being selfish or greedy."

"Being jealous, or always wanting to be first," Chris added.

"Those are all good answers. Probably you can think of a lot more, too." Uncle Roger patted Chris and Emma on the shoulder and continued, "All those things are like the poison in the cone shell, aren't they? They hurt other people around us. So even though the cone may be very beautiful outside, its beauty is only skin deep."

"Or shell-deep," laughed Chris.

"Right," Uncle Roger smiled. "Meanwhile, inside, the animal is full of ugliness. So if we want to be beautiful on the inside, what should we be like?" he asked.

"Kind," Danielle answered before anyone else.
"Loving," Emma said, "and sharing with others."
"Polite and respectful," said Chris. "Honest, too; not lying or cheating."
"Good," Uncle Roger said. "What else?"
"Obey Mommy and Daddy," Danielle said.
"Don't be proud and boast about how good you are," Chris added.
"Be helpful and patient," Emma suggested.
Chris had another idea. "Be forgiving, too."

Uncle Roger smiled again at the children, then he looked at Mama and said, "It looks like you're going to have some beautiful children if they remember all these things!"

Mama thought for a moment, then asked the children, "Remember working in the garden a few days ago? It's better to be like our ugly little earthworms that are so helpful, isn't it, rather than to be like these beautiful cone shells with their ugly, deadly habits?!"

"That makes me think of another Bible verse," said Daddy. "This time from the first book of Peter, chapter five and verse eight. It basically says, 'Watch out! Be careful! Satan is your enemy, and he is going around like a roaring lion, trying to find someone to swallow up!'"

Satan wants to "poison" our thoughts and our actions so that we act like the ugly sting of the cone shell … but Jesus wants to help make us beautiful in everything we say and do.

True Beauty

They say that true beauty
Is only "skin deep,"
But goodness of heart
You always can keep.

Some cone shells are pretty
When you look at the shell
But inside they're ugly,
And deadly as well.
Some people are like that –

They look nice outside;
But if you look closely,
They're not nice inside.

Some may be selfish,
Or quite impolite;
Some get angry quickly –
Just ready to fight.
Some lie and they cheat,
Or always act proud;
Some may be quite bossy,
And pushy and loud.

But it's beautiful inside
That we need to be.
By our words and our actions,
Other people will see
That we're kind and we're loving,
We are helpful and caring,
We're obedient always,
Unselfish and sharing.

If we're polite and respectful,
Patient, forgiving,
We'll have true inner beauty
And bless others by living.

The Hidden Destroyers

Chris opened the cupboard door and pulled a book from the shelf which he had not looked at for many months. As he opened it … oh, no! Something had been chewing up the paper inside the front cover!

What was it? Mama wasn't sure what had eaten the paper in Chris's book. But one thing was certain: *something* was spoiling it.

Another day Emma came rushing into Mama's room with some very important news. "Mama, do you know what Janelle told me? She said there is an old warehouse close to our house. Nobody is there anymore, and she got lots of books there … free! May we go see, Mama? Please, may we?"

"Now, what are you talking about, Emma?" Mama asked. "Where is this? Are you sure it is okay to go inside?"

Emma kept talking about the books and the warehouse, and Mama finally understood which building she meant. Mama said that she would ask for permission, and then, that weekend, they could go and take a look.

In just a few minutes, they came to the old building. All of the doors were open wide.

When the weekend arrived, Emma didn't forget. "Mama, let's go to the warehouse today. Remember? You promised! May Janelle come too?"

So Mama, Emma, and Janelle walked down a path and through a grassy field. In just a few minutes, they came to the old building. All of the doors were open wide. Mama looked inside, then they all walked into the back storeroom. There on the floor was a big pile of children's books.

They were terribly dusty, but Mama carefully picked up the top book. On its golden cover were pictures of ships and sailboats, animals and adventures. It contained stories of sportsmen, inventors, and discoverers. Mama thought that Chris and Danielle would enjoy this book, so she put it to one side. Then she picked up the next one, which had a green cover and a different title.

But when she opened it, she did not find a lot of interesting stories. Instead, she found a hollow shell with a few little animals that looked like ants crawling around inside. "Termites!" she exclaimed.

Emma and Mama picked up several more books. Some had golden-yellow covers, some blue, some green. Others had no more than a front cover. However, only that first book, from the very top of the stack, could ever be read. All of the rest had been completely ruined by the termites.

"Termites, which some people call 'white ants,' are great tunnel makers," said Mama. "They eat paths through trees, the wood in buildings, and furniture. They eat cloth and books and paper."

Emma wrinkled up her nose at the thought.

Mama continued, "Some kinds build large mounds, or towers, of dirt. When I went to Cambodia to help for a few days, I saw several that were about three feet tall. But in places like Africa, the mounds may grow into 'skyscrapers' almost thirty feet tall!

"Inside a mound," Mama said, "the queen is busy laying as many as 80,000 eggs every day. That is nearly one every second!"

"Wow! That's a *lot!*" exclaimed Janelle.

"Many kinds of termites live in fallen trees," Mama said. "They chew up the dead wood and recycle it back into the soil." She smiled. "These sorts are very helpful.

"The biggest problem with termites," Mama went on, "is that they can ruin many things before anyone ever realizes that they are there. One kind – the type that causes us real problems – is called a 'subterranean' termite. That word means that they usually build their nests under the ground. The problem is that they do not stay there. Instead, they go exploring in buildings, entering through tiny little cracks. That is when the real trouble begins!"

A bit disappointed at not having some "new" books to take home with them, the girls put the ones they had looked at back onto the pile and headed for home.

One afternoon not much later, Emma and Danielle went with Mama to visit Auntie Sara and Uncle Daniel, who were busy cleaning the house their family had just rented. On the way, Mama said how nice it would be for Auntie Sara and Uncle Daniel to live in a place that was truly big enough for their family. It also had a nice yard, she said, where their boys, Jonathan, Jeffery, and Jimmy, could play. It was quite an old house, though; and oh, what a mess it was!

When they arrived, Auntie Sara opened the kitchen cupboards, and they all saw the thin lines of dried mud everywhere. Auntie said, "When I first opened the bedroom closets, I found mud trails on the walls. And when I opened the drawers … yes, you guessed it! More muddy lines. There are hundreds of tunnels in this house, made by millions of termites!" Then she took Mama and the girls to look in the bedrooms.

When they came into one of them, Danielle saw Uncle Daniel standing near the top of a big ladder. Right in front of him, above the window, there was a nicely-painted white board covering the hole where an air conditioner had once been.

"Mommy, what is Uncle Daniel doing?" Danielle asked.

"I'm not sure," Mama answered. "You'd better ask him."

Danielle was about to do just that when they heard a big, long *crack!* She and Emma jumped, frightened by the noise.

Jonathan and Jeffery came running in from the next room. "What happened, Daddy?" they asked at the same time.

At first Uncle Daniel looked surprised, but then he just smiled and shook his head. In his hands he held the white board. All over him, and all over the floor, were bits of dirt and dried mud. Slowly he turned the board around so that everyone could see it.

Thousands of tiny termites raced around on it, surprised to see daylight, because they always live in the darkness, hidden away where nobody sees them. That white board, which had looked very nice on the outside, did not look so nice on the inside! Instead, it had tunnels going in all directions.

When Uncle Daniel dropped the board on the floor, it broke into several pieces. It had been completely ruined by all the termites.

☙ ✦ ❧

That is the way termites work: they leave everything on the outside looking normal and nice while they are busy destroying the inside. Eventually a wall, a door, or even a whole porch may tumble down.

And this is exactly the same way that bad habits work in our lives. Some children begin to smoke or drink alcohol or use drugs. These habits are like termites, damaging the body. The harm may not show at first, but finally the person's life and health are destroyed, and by then it may be too late to help.

There are other habits, too, which work quietly on the inside. Lying, cheating, bullying, hurting others, stealing, and many other actions may not *look* like they are causing any problem. Boys and girls may get away with their bad habits for a long time. However, little bad habits when one is young become big bad habits once one is older.

The time to break those bad habits is now, so that they don't cause real damage. Remember: just as the termites ruined the books and boards, bad habits can spoil your whole life.

The Spoilers

Those little termite spoilers
Are difficult to see,
And yet they're doing their damage
As busily as can be.
And so it is with habits bad:
They may seem fun at first,
But when they get control of you,
They'll leave you at your worst!
You may not see what they are doing
Until the harm is great,
So stop those harmful habits now—
Don't wait till it's too late.

Don't Be a Chameleon!

"See that lizard there in the mud?" Daddy called to the children at the park one afternoon. All three hurried along the wooden pathway to where he was standing and looked to see what he was pointing at.

"Where, Daddy?" Emma wanted to know. Daddy pointed at it again, but "it" was hard to see.

Chris was the first to exclaim, "I see it! Right there!" Finally Emma saw it too.

But Danielle was still having trouble. "I can't find it, Daddy. Where is it?" she complained.

Mama tried to help. "Just look right beside that little mud hill." Then she laughed, "At first I thought it was just an old stick of wood! It really has good camouflage."

"Good what?" Danielle asked.

"Camouflage," Chris answered her. "That means his color is just like the ground or tree that he's standing on. Like soldiers' uniforms that are the same colors as the jungle plants."

"That's right, Chris," Mama said. "Camouflage is an animal's natural protection against its enemies. It matches the place where it is sitting, sometimes with spots or stripes or other patterns."

"Like the baby deer?" asked Danielle.

"Yes, like little fawns," Mama answered.

"Sometimes they change colors, like the chameleon," Emma added.

Danielle pulled on Daddy's arm. "Come on, let's go. I'm tired of just standing."

Everyone resumed walking on down the path, but Daddy kept talking about lizards. "Remember the last time I went to meetings up north with Mr. Smith? A tree had fallen across the road near the hotel where we were going to stay, so we had to stop. Some men with power saws were busy cutting the tree into smaller pieces so that they could move it off of the road. I knew that we would have to wait for a few minutes, so I got out of the car and walked around near the other end of the tree where they were not cutting.

"When the road was cleared enough so that we could get through, I got back into the car, and we drove on to the hotel. As I was sitting in the car, I looked down at my lap. Suddenly I noticed a small lizard sitting very, very still, right near my knee. I had not seen him at first because the color and the pattern of his skin had changed to match my pants.

"He remained right where he was until we reached the hotel a few minutes later. Even as I got out of the car and started to walk toward the hotel with my suitcase, he stayed on his new 'tree' … my leg! On the way in, I stopped to talk with some of the other people who were there for the same meetings. Pretty soon I felt the lizard crawling up the back of my neck. Then he climbed right onto my head."

"Oh, no!" Danielle laughed.

Daddy continued, "I decided that that was enough, so I gently brushed him off, and he quickly ran away."

Danielle giggled some more, then she looked at Daddy's pants to see if there might be another one on him now. Meanwhile Daddy continued to talk about lizards.

"Besides camouflage," he told them, "lizards have another good protection from their enemies. Have you ever tried to catch one? If you caught it by the tail, what would happen?"

"It would fall off!" Chris and Emma answered at the same time.

"Yes, the tail would stay in your hand, and the lizard would run away! Many kinds of lizards can drop their tails when caught by an enemy. And the tail continues to move for several minutes, so the enemy often keeps watching it while the lizard escapes."

Daddy added, "Did you know that there are almost 4,000 different kinds of lizards? They don't live in the Arctic or the Antarctic where it is so very cold, but they live just about everywhere else in the world."

Mama thought that the worst place for them to live was in the house, and said so. "The little gecko is the most common lizard to find inside," she said. "I do like having them catch mosquitos that come into the house, but there are some things I do not like. For example, one day, Daddy opened the refrigerator and found a dead baby gecko inside."

"Oh, yuck!" Danielle said.

"Another day Chris went to get something from the freezer, and guess what he saw?" Mama asked. "A frozen gecko! But maybe the worst time was when Auntie Sydney was helping me to clean out the toaster and found a very dried-up and toasted gecko. She wouldn't eat toasted bread at our house for a long time after that!" For Mama, however, that still wasn't the worst thing about those little lizards.

Lizard, lizard, on the wall,
Please be careful not to fall.

She told the children, "Because their flat toes have thousands of tiny hairs with hooks on the ends, the little geckos in the house can run all over the walls and even on the ceilings." She went on, "That would be okay if they always stayed there, but four different times a gecko let go of the wall or doorway just as I was walking through!"

Daddy said, "Maybe you can imagine what happened. *Bump!* The gecko landed right on Mama's head or shoulder! Now, she was quite brave, and she didn't scream as some ladies would."

"I did make a big squeak every time it happened, though," Mama admitted, "and I always shiver when I think about it."

Daddy teased her, "You should just be thankful they were only tiny geckos instead of Komodo dragons!"

Mama really did shiver at the thought about having one of those big fellows near her. She explained to the children, "Komodo dragons may be as much as ten feet long. And some of them weigh more than 300 pounds!"

Daddy thought about Mama's experiences, and soon he came up with a little poem that went like this:

Lizard, lizard, on the wall,
Please be careful not to fall.
For if you fall, I fear you'll be
Landing right on top of me!

That evening when the family got home from the park, Mama was still thinking about lizards. At dinner time she said, "This afternoon we talked about chameleons. How far can each of you stick out your tongue?"

All three children tried to see who could stick their tongue out the farthest.

"So short!" Mama teased them. "Did you know that a chameleon's tongue is longer than the distance from its nose to the tip of its tail? To get food, the chameleon just sits or else creeps quietly, always watching for an insect or a spider. Then, *zap!* As quick as a flash, that long, sticky tongue shoots out to catch some dinner!"

"Now try this trick," Daddy said. "I want you to look at Mama sitting down at that end of the table."

They all did as he asked, then Daddy spoke again, "Okay, now I want you to look over here at me at the same time."

The three children started looking cross-eyed and making funny faces, trying to look in both directions at once. Then they all began to laugh at each other. "That's impossible!" Chris told Daddy.

"Well, for you it's impossible," Daddy smiled, "but not for the chameleon. Your eyes work together, but theirs can work separately. That way, they can look in any two directions that they want to at the same time."

"That must really help with their hunting!" Emma exclaimed.

Meanwhile, Mama was thinking about something else. "The way they change colors is still the most interesting thing to me. First of all, a chameleon changes colors to tell other chameleons what kind of mood it is in. If it is angry, its face will probably turn black."

"Is that why some people say that a person's face is black when they are angry?" Chris wanted to know.

"Maybe so," Mama smiled. "Secondly, a chameleon changes according to time and place. After dark, its color usually changes to yellow. During the day, its skin turns different shades of green or brown. That color may be light or dark, depending on what it is sitting on. Its skin may even be patchy or spotty to match where it is sitting."

"Like the camouflage we were talking about," Emma added.

"That's right, Emma." Mama answered. "You know, sometimes children – or even big people – are like chameleons. They're afraid to be different; they want to be just like everyone else."

"I know, just like Emma. She always wants to have a dress exactly like Angela's," Chris grumbled. "She has to have the same book Angela has. Or if Angela is going swimming, Emma wants to go swimming. If Angela – "

Emma interrupted, "You always want to play the same games, and watch the same videos, and wear the same kind of shoes as all of your friends."

"Now, wait a minute; let's not have a big fight, here," Mama warned. "But that is what I was talking about: wanting to be just like other people, and never wanting to be different. It is fine to follow what is honest and good. But sometimes the group wants to do something that isn't the best. Then what will you do?"

"I know," said Emma thoughtfully. "Remember, Mama, when I told you about Jennifer and Natalie wanting me to steal some things from the store on the way home from school? Every day they told me about what they had taken, and they kept asking me to come with them."

"I remember, Emma," answered Mama. "That is what we call 'peer pressure.' Your peers are your friends, schoolmates, or other people your age, and peer pressure is when they try to make you do something just because they are doing it."

"That's why a lot of boys and girls begin to smoke cigarettes," said Daddy, "or start other bad habits. Because 'everyone else is doing it.' But just because others are doing it doesn't mean you have to. You don't have to be a chameleon that looks or acts just like everyone else around!"

"Don't let peer pressure make you do anything that you shouldn't do." Mama continued. "It is very important to learn how to just say '*No*' and really mean it. For example, you children each have your own hobbies. Chris, you like to collect marbles and work on the computer. Emma enjoys drawing and cooking. Danielle collects sea shells and loves her pets. When the other kids want you to do something that isn't so good, just tell them you have other things you want to do instead."

"You all have your special talents and abilities, too," Daddy added. "Danielle is doing well with her piano lessons. I know that Emma is making some very good speeches at school and plays the clarinet well. Chris is a very good student and already very good at the trombone. And each of you enjoys some kind of sports. Just keep working on those talents, and become someone special in what *you* are good at instead of trying to be like everyone else."

"If you want to copy someone," Mama said, "learn more about Jesus and copy Him."

"So, Danni," Daddy asked, "what was Jesus like?"

"He loved people," she answered.

"He obeyed God all the time," said Chris.

"And He was patient and didn't get mad all the time," Emma added.

"Those are all good answers," Mama said. "He was also kind and helpful, wasn't He? By learning from God's Word, the Bible, Jesus knew what would make His Father happy. Jesus also prayed a lot, and asked His Father to always show Him what He should do. So, even if people tried to make Him do wrong things, those two things – reading the Bible and praying – helped Jesus to always do what was right."

Just Be Yourself

You don't need to be
Exactly like me;
And I need not do
The same things as you.
So I'll just be me,
And you just be you.
But let's all be like Jesus!

Monkey See, Monkey Do

One Sunday morning, Mama called out from her room, "Danni, come here. Hurry!" As Danielle came through the door, Mama then whispered, "Shh, come quietly to the window."

Not far away from the house, they saw three monkeys swinging through the trees. There was a father, a mother, and her baby holding on tightly to her back. "They must have just come into the neighborhood," Mama said softly. "We've never seen them around the house before." Excited, Danielle called Emma and Chris to see the new visitors.

For some time after that, it was lots of fun to watch the monkeys play in the trees and swing on the telephone line. Then one day Chris called Mama, Emma, and Danielle to look out the kitchen window. "Look up there," Chris said as he pointed to the tall tree on the other side of their yard. As Mama and the children watched, each monkey took one or two bites out of a mango, then let it drop to the ground. They each bit another mango, and then another, and another, until almost all of the mangoes were ruined.

On another day, while she was outside, Danielle observed the biggest monkey taking notice of Mama and Daddy's car. He walked back and forth across the hood, leaving dirty footprints on the white paint. Then he tried to look at himself in the side mirror. Danielle laughed. "What a silly animal." she said to herself. After watching for a minute or two, she called Chris and Emma out to watch the monkey show.

However, after a few weeks passed, Daddy was not laughing at the monkey's actions anymore. Besides making the car dirty, the monkey was also clawing at the rubber around the windshield.

Every day Emma checked to see how much more was missing. "Those monkeys will have to go!" Daddy announced one day, after the monkey had done more damage to the car. He went right to the telephone and asked Mr. Wong to bring the cage trap so they could catch the monkeys and take them away.

Soon Mr. Wong caught the baby, and he took it to a lake a few miles from their house to set it free. It wasn't long before the father monkey was also caught, and it went to the lake, too. It turned out that the mother was not so easy to catch, but before long, everyone forgot about trying. She didn't seem to be causing any problems, anyway.

A few months later, however, trouble began again. Some of the neighbors were feeding the monkey, and it was getting bolder all the time. Finally the monkey got so brave that it started to chase Danielle.

That big monkey would sit on the roof or sidewalk right near the door, and every time Danielle tried to go outside to play, the monkey would chase her right back into the house. Sometimes Chris laughed when he saw the monkey chasing her (big brothers aren't always as kind as they should be), but poor little Danielle did not think it was funny. She became afraid to ever go out and play.

At last Mama asked Mr. Wong to set the trap again and catch the troublemaker, but he still did not have any luck catching that monkey. Then one day Mama's friend Andrew came to visit.

Mama told him about the trouble they had been having with the monkey, and he set the trap with a nice bunch of bananas inside.

That big monkey would sit on the roof or sidewalk right near the door, and every time Danielle tried to go outside to play, the monkey would chase her right back into the house.

Mama, Danielle, and Andrew went into the house and sat down, watching out the window to see what would happen. Since monkeys are very curious, it was only a few minutes before, *bang!*: there was the naughty monkey, caught in the cage.

Mama phoned Mr. Wong, and just a little while later, he came and took the caged mother monkey to the lake. He set her free in the jungle there, where she wouldn't bother anyone. And Danielle was happy to be able to play outside again without a monkey chasing her!

One evening soon after that, Daddy started talking about monkeys again. "You know," he said, "besides being curious, a monkey is also very clever: it is smart enough to find out how to get whatever it wants. The monkey is also quite tricky and dishonest, however."

He began telling about something that had happened when he and his sister were in seventh grade. "When Auntie Doe and I were kids, we had to ride the train ride for hundreds of miles to get to our boarding school up in the high Himalayan mountains of north India. For our trip, Grandma J had packed some food for us, but I also bought some bananas at a train station along the way.

"Later in the morning," Daddy continued, "while the train was stopped at a different station, Auntie Doe decided to eat one of the bananas. Sitting there in her train seat, she peeled the skin back and started to take a bite.

Suddenly, a big hairy hand reached in between the bars on the window and grabbed the banana right out of her hand. Auntie Doe screamed, but the monkey was gone. So was the banana!"

"Yes, sometimes monkeys can be very naughty!" Mama said. "And we may laugh at the bad things they do, but I really hope that none of us will act like them. It is better to be like the monkeys that use their minds to choose to do good things."

☙ ❖ ❧

Monkeys belong to a big family called "primates." The primates include a lot of monkey-like animals, such as lemurs, baboons, gorillas, orangutans, chimpanzees, and macaques.

Macaques can be taught how to pick coconuts from high up in trees. They climb to the top, twist a coconut until it falls off the stem, and then drop it onto the ground. Did you know that a well-trained macaque can pick as many as 500 coconuts in one day? Then it helps its trainer to carry them and put them into a cart.

Another primate, the chimpanzee, sometimes goes to a special school. A few have learned to use some of the same sign language as deaf people. One chimp, after living with people for more than ten years, learned to sign 120 words with his hands.

A famous gorilla, Koko, also learned sign language. Koko learned how to sign more than 500 words. Koko even had a pet kitten and would use sign language to "talk" about it. She tried to take good care of the kitten: she would hold it, brush its fur, and patiently let the kitten crawl all over her.

Most primates (including Koko) learn to do things by copying what they see. One time some men were building a new road through a jungle. Suddenly they came to a clear area with several bonfires, all waiting to be lit. They wondered who had piled up the wood so neatly, because no people lived anywhere nearby.

The workers watched for a long time. Finally they saw a monkey come out of the jungle and neatly place some more wood on one of the piles. The men realized that the monkeys must have seen people build fires before: they were just copying what they had seen.

Sometimes children are like monkeys: they copy what they see other people do. That is good *if* you always copy what is right and honest. For example, it is nice to be like the helpful macaques or like the kind and gentle gorilla, Koko.

We know from the Bible that Jesus loved us very, very much. And He told us that we should love other people and do good to them, in just the same way as He did for us. He never, ever did anything wrong or unkind.

His life was an example to us, showing us how to live. Jesus wants us to never copy those people who do bad or mean things, but instead to copy Him in everything we do.

Copycat

I've heard people say
"Monkey see, monkey do."
Would it be good – or bad –
If I copied you?

Trapped!

As soon as she got home from school, Emma sat right down to do her homework. Soon she had finished everything except her science. She got up from her chair and went to find Mama. "Mama, could you help me with my science project?" Emma asked. "On Thursday I have to give a report about spiders. I got some books from the library, but I don't think that's enough."

"We have the nature books that Grandma has given you," Mama said, "and maybe we can borrow some more from Auntie Maria. Why don't you give her a call and ask if she will let you borrow some?"

Emma hurried to the telephone, and soon returned to Mama's side. "Auntie Maria said we could come over and get them now if we want to. May we, Mama?"

On the way, Mama and Emma talked about the report. "After dinner this evening, maybe we can get Daddy and Chris to help," Mama suggested. "We can all have some fun finding out more about spiders."

That evening Emma brought together all the materials she had collected. Danielle enjoyed looking at some of the pictures while Chris, Emma, Mama, and Daddy started searching for interesting information.

"Here's something," said Chris. "All together there are more than 30,000 kinds of spiders."

"Wow, that's a lot!" exclaimed Emma in surprise.

"Here's something your teacher will expect you to know," said Mama. "Spiders are not insects. Instead, they belong to the group of animals called 'arachnids.' They don't have any wings or antennae, and their bodies are divided into two parts. Their head and chest are in the front part, and the abdomen is in the back part."

"Do you know the size of the smallest and largest spiders?" asked Daddy. "Some are only as big as the head of a pin. Some of the largest spiders are certain tarantulas, which can be as big as a man's hand."

"Ooh, those must be scary!" Emma said. She shivered just thinking about such big spiders.

"Not really," Chris replied. "I remember when we lived at the farm when I was Danni's age; in the autumn we'd see lots of tarantulas crossing the road. We don't see them much anymore, but Tyler always tries to find one when he's at the farm in the autumn."

Emma spoke again, "It says here that all spiders can make silk, but they don't all use it for spinning webs. At their tail end, they have little tubes called 'spin … ' how do you say this, Mama?" she asked.

"Spin-ner-ets … spinnerets," Mama helped her.

"Spiders use the silk for a lot of different things," Emma continued. "Some make webs to catch their food. Some wrap their eggs in silk until the babies hatch, like the wolf spider, which carries its eggs around in a silk sack."

"This book talks about webs, too," Daddy added. "Did you know that spider silk is stronger than a steel thread of the same size? And the webs can also stretch a lot."

"Remember those spider webs out at the park?" Chris asked. "When we pushed on them gently, they wouldn't even break."

"Those were made by orb spiders," Mama told them. "They make their webs in such a pretty design: their webs look like the spokes of a bicycle tire, with circles going round and round. Insects that touch those webs get stuck to the silk threads. Then they're caught! As soon as the spider feels his web move, he comes running. Then he poisons the insect and eats it."

"Here's something that's hard to believe," Chris said. "In one grassy field the size of a baseball or football field, there may be 100,000 spiders."

"Remember all those webs we saw in the grass at the park the other day?" Mama asked. "There certainly were a lot of them in just a little area."

"Wouldn't it be harmful to have so many spiders on a farm?" Emma questioned.

"Oh, no," Daddy answered. "Without all those spiders catching bugs for dinner, there would be way too many insects. It's the insects which damage the crops. So in fact, most spiders are very helpful to farmers, just like earthworms."

"I remember Uncle Henrik saying that a house with spiders is a healthy house," Mama remembered. She continued, "Look at this photograph. Do you see a spider anywhere?"

Everyone looked at the picture Mama was holding. There were green leaves all around what looked like a large, lovely, pink-and-white flower. There were also several small, pink flower buds … but no one saw a spider.

Finally Mama laughed. "That big, pink 'flower' is really a crab spider," she told them.

"Why is it called that?" Chris wondered.

"Because it moves sideways like the real crabs down at the beach," Mama answered. "Many crab spiders have very good camouflage. Do you remember what camouflage is?" she asked.

There were green leaves all around what looked like a large, lovely, pink-and-white flower.

"I do," answered Danielle quickly. "They look like soldiers!"

Chris looked at Danielle and said, "Silly, they don't look like soldiers! Soldiers wear camouflage colors so that they look like the jungle. And chameleons change colors so that they look like the tree or whatever they are standing on."

"Now, Chris," Daddy spoke. "Don't make fun of Danni. I think that's what she meant. Actually, I think both of you are correct. Camouflage is looking like what is around you, isn't it?"

Mama continued, "As I was saying, many of the crab spiders look like the place where they like to live and catch their food. This pink one lives on pink flowers. Yellow crab spiders live on yellow flowers, green ones on green plants, and so on."

"What would happen if you moved the pink spider to a yellow flower?" Chris wanted to know.

"Apparently the scientists wondered the same thing, Chris," Mama said. "Guess what happened when they put the spiders on wrong-colored flowers?"

"They changed colors!" Danielle answered.

"Good guess, Danni," said Mama, "but not the crab spiders. Instead, they hurried to find flowers that matched them!

"On a right-colored flower, a crab spider sits very, very still, waiting for

a little insect to come along. When the bug is close enough, the spider grabs it. Then he bites it, poisoning it so that it cannot move. After that, the spider sucks the juices out of the insect."

As Chris looked through magazine articles, he found something interesting. "It tells here about jumping spiders. They watch their prey just like a cat does, then, when the insect comes close enough, they jump onto it."

"What happens if a spider misses the insect? Does he just fall down?" Emma wanted to know.

"No, because before it jumps, it spins a silk safety line," Chris answered. "It glues that to the place where it is sitting. That way, if it misses his target, the line holds it in the air, and it can climb back up to where it was." Chris turned to his little sister and asked, "Hey, Danni, do you know how far a jumping spider can jump?"

"How far?" Danielle asked.

"This says that it can jump as far as ten inches. That doesn't sound like much, but if Emma and I could jump as well as the jumping spider, we could go more than thirty feet!"

"Wow!" Daddy exclaimed. "That's all the way across our kitchen and dining room!"

"Here's another interesting way of catching your food: spit at it!" Emma laughed, and so did everyone else. "That's what the spitting spider does. It waits until the insect comes close enough, then it spits silk at it. The poor insect gets glued to the ground, and the spider can slowly walk over to eat its dinner!"

Everyone was quiet for some time, then Daddy spoke. "We've seen a lot of ways that spiders catch their prey. All of them use some kind of a trap. Usually the trap looks harmless, and sometimes it is even quite pretty to look at. Right?"

The children nodded their heads in agreement.

"There are a lot of traps in life for boys and girls, and for adults as well," Daddy said. "Traps like smoking cigarettes, drinking alcohol, taking drugs, gambling, cheating, stealing and such things."

"Remember how we talked about 'peer pressure' recently?" Mama asked. "Don't ever let your friends, schoolmates, or anyone dare you or get you to do something if you don't think it is right. For instance, they may tell you that gambling is fun, and that you can win money that way. What they won't tell you is that by gambling you are more likely to lose money … and happiness. In the past two months, I've heard about three families in which the parents divorced because of gambling."

Daddy went on, "Someone may tell you that smoking is the popular or grown-up thing to do."

"They may tell you that you're a scaredy-cat if you don't smoke!" Chris suggested.

"Why not offer them some lung cancer, and see if they're a 'scaredy-cat' to reject that!" Mama asked. "Besides, what is popular or grown-up about getting lung cancer?"

"If you don't smoke, or steal, or whatever your friends want you to do," said Emma, "they'll say that you can't be part of their group."

"Of course," Daddy pointed out, "if you die of lung cancer from smoking, or if you land in jail for stealing, you won't be part of the group anyway! So don't fall into their traps."

"Daddy mentioned drugs," added Mama. "Many people start taking drugs at parties or because some friend tells them it is exciting and fun. What a trap that is! Some people's lives are ruined the very first time they try drugs. Others just slowly spoil their bodies or minds." Mama paused. "Oh, no," she said, "I think we got off the subject of spiders!"

Emma looked at the paper on which she was writing all the ideas and thought for a moment. "I think I will tell about people-traps in my report, too," she decided. "Thanks, everyone, for all of your help."

❦

Beware!

Remember Miss Muffet who sat on a tuffet
And was afraid of the spider that sat down beside her?
Many people today feel just the same way.
Though most spiders don't bite, we still are a-fright.
But we don't need to fear – there's reason for cheer:
Those spiders help eat harmful insects they meet.
Whether he jumps or spits, or in his web just sits,
Each spider can zap his food by some trap.
But it's not just the spider that has its traps hid;
Life has its traps, too, for children like you.
There are traps everywhere, just waiting to snare,
But if you'll stay alert, you will not get hurt.
When friends say to smoke, or take drugs – that stuff's no joke! –
Or they ask you to drink, you'd best stop and think.
Just learn to say "no," and let those friends know
That your life and your health are your greatest wealth.
Life's too precious to lose, so make sure that you choose
To enjoy what is best and stay away from the rest.
When such dangers come near, you don't need to fear,
Just be like Miss Muffet, who ran from her tuffet …
And quickly run away!

The Voice of Instinct

The children were sitting in the back seat of the Volkswagen Beetle. Chris and Emma were eager to get home after riding for almost two hours. Little Danielle had already fallen asleep.

Only a few miles from home, Daddy suddenly stepped on the brake and stopped the car. That brought Chris and Emma to attention. "What's the matter, Daddy?" they asked at almost the same time.

"Didn't you see what was on the road back there?" Daddy asked them.

"No," they answered. Mother hadn't seen it either and was as curious as the children. As Daddy carefully backed the car toward his secret, both Chris and Emma watched out the back window. Emma exclaimed once she saw what it was: "Look, a turtle!"

Daddy stopped the car, got out, and walked toward the brownish-green turtle in the middle of the narrow road. As he got closer, the turtle quickly pulled its head and legs into its shell to hide.

Daddy reached down to pick it up. "Hmm," he thought aloud, "this must be about ten inches across. He's a big one." Then Daddy walked back to the car and gently put the turtle on the floor by Emma's feet.

"Ahh!" she screeched and pulled her feet up onto the seat. "Don't put him here, Daddy!" she begged. But Emma really didn't need to worry: the poor turtle was just as afraid as she was, and kept its head inside its shell for the rest of the ride.

Once they were home, Daddy carefully lifted the turtle out of the car and placed it on the grass. "Bring some water, Chris," he said.

Soon Chris brought back a bucket and poured a little water onto the turtle's back. Then he and Emma stood nearby and watched to see what it would do … but that turtle didn't do anything! It just stayed still with its head tucked into its shell.

Finally, Daddy told them to move far away from the turtle so it wouldn't be afraid. Chris and Emma quickly obeyed, walking over to the back porch. There they sat down quietly to watch.

At last the turtle peeked out of the shell. It looked around slowly, carefully, to see if there was any danger. For a few more minutes the turtle just sat there with its nose up in the air. Then it turned and started walking, slowly, straight toward the safety of a little canal across the grassy field.

Several more times after that, Daddy found turtles on his way home. Each time, the turtle was very shy at first. Yet eventually the turtle would always seem to sniff the air with its head held high. Then it would slowly turn and head toward the same little canal.

On a later evening, Daddy observed, "Somehow the turtles always seemed to know which way to go to find water."

Mama then told the children, "Actually, it probably was not such a good thing for Daddy to bring the turtles home. Even though he was very gentle with them, land turtles like to stay within a certain area. Did you know that most of them never go more than about a mile or two from their home?"

"That's true," Daddy said. "Sea turtles lay their eggs on a sandy beach. When the eggs hatch, those babies go out to sea. Then, when it is time to lay their eggs, they always return to the same beach where they began life."

Mama spoke again. "Turtles have something special that many animals have. It is called 'instinct.' Instinct is what tells the land turtle which way to go to find the water. It tells the sea turtle which beach to go back to when the time comes to lay her eggs. Can you think of some other examples of instinct?" she asked.

"Yes," answered Emma. "Instinct teaches a baby kangaroo to crawl into its mother's pouch."

"Instinct also helps a baby chick to peck its way out of the eggshell at just the right time," Chris added. "And it helps birds know how to build the right kind of nests."

"Danni," Mother asked, "what does instinct teach a caterpillar?"

"To make a cocoon?"

"That's right!" Mama answered. "And it helps spiders know what kind of web to spin, doesn't it?"

"You're all right," said Daddy. "Although boys and girls do not seem to have much in the way of instinct, you do have something which is just as important: something called 'conscience.' It is like a little voice in your head which tells you what is right and what is wrong.

"When an animal follows its instinct, it will always do what it is supposed to do. In just the same way, if you listen to the little voice of conscience speaking in your mind, telling you to do what is right, you will always do what is best, too."

"That reminds me of a song about reading the Bible," Mama said. "The Bible is God's Word, telling us how to live so that we do not sin. Danni, do you know what 'sin' is?"

"Being bad," she answered.

"That's right. It means not obeying God's rules," Mama said. "Here are the words to the song." And she sang,

Thy Word have I hid in my heart
That I might not sin against Thee;
That I might not sin, that I might not sin.
Thy Word have I hid in my heart.[5]

"That's a good song to sing often," said Daddy. "And if we learn from the Bible what God wants us to do, that is how we can make sure that the little voice of our conscience is always ready to be our instinct."

The Little Voice

Instinct helps a turtle know
Where it was born, which way to go.
It helps the birds up in the sky
Know where to go and when to fly.
It helps the baby kangaroo
Find mother's pouch to crawl into.
Instinct is for bears and squirrels,
But conscience is for boys and girls.
It's like a voice inside of you
That tells you what you ought to do.
If you'll obey it day and night,
You will always do what's right.

---

[5] Ernest O Sellers, "Thy Word Have I Hid in My Heart," 1908, Public Domain.

The Kay-Nines

"Daddy, may we get a puppy?" Danielle asked at dinner one evening.

"Do you really think you need one? After all, you already have a cat and all these birds," Daddy answered.

"But Cocky is Mommy's bird," Danielle said. "Besides, they don't play with me like a puppy would."

Chris spoke up, "Oh, Mom, Danni has so many pets already that she can hardly take care of all of them!"

"I don't want any dog if we can't have Colonel back," Emma said sadly. "What if Daddy gets moved again? I never want to have to say goodbye to another dog."

"But I was too little to play with Colonel. I want a dog that *I* can play with," Danielle complained.

Mama saw that Danielle's mood was getting worse every minute, so she decided to change the subject a little. "Danni, did you know that not all dogs are for playing with?"

Danielle didn't quite know how to answer that question, so she said nothing.

"Haven't you seen those K-9 pickup trucks sometimes?" Chris asked his sister.

"Kay … nine? What's that?" Danielle wanted to know.

"They write it with the letter 'k' and the number nine," Chris explained to his little sister, "but it really means 'canine,' spelled c-a-n-i-n-e. That's the scientific name for dogs. Anyway, the K-9 pickups take dogs out for guard duty. They work as watchdogs at places like shopping centers, banks, and prisons."

"They may do other kinds of work, too," Mama added.

"I know something else that dogs do," Emma spoke up. "I read in some of my books that they guide blind people."

"That's right," Mama answered with a big smile on her face. "Did you know that I had a blind piano teacher when I was about your age, Emma? He had a guide dog."

"Really?" Emma and Danielle asked at once.

"Yes. Mr. Good was probably the best piano teacher I ever had. I always enjoyed watching and listening to him play. He was really good. In the daytime he gave lessons, and in the evenings he played at a restaurant downtown. Everywhere he went, that dog went with him."

"What kind of dog was it? A German Shepherd like I saw in the pictures?" asked Danielle.

Mama nodded and said, "Yes, and it was *big!* I used to be afraid of it. When I went for my lessons, the dog would bark before I even got near the door. When Mr. Good opened the door, the dog was always by his side. Then when we walked over to the piano, Mr. Good would sit on one side of me, while the dog sat on the other – right next to me – watching every

move I made. It was really protecting its master!" Mama shivered as she thought about it.

Danielle suddenly thought about another dog. "Mommy, do you remember when we went on the airplane to Los Angeles, and we saw the cute little brown-and-white doggy in the airport? You said it was working. What was it doing, Mommy?"

"Yes, I remember," Mama answered. "That was a pretty little beagle, and it was sniffing for drugs. A lot of big airports use dogs to check for bad drugs that people are carrying."

Emma had another story to tell. "When Auntie Melanee took Tyler to the doctor the other day, there was a nice dog there. It was a German Shepherd and Chow mix named Rocky. The doctor got him when he was just a puppy, and she has had him for six or seven years already. She taught Rocky to be a friend to the children who come into her office.

Emma continued, "The nurse said that when Rocky and the doctor first come to the office in the morning, one of the ladies gives Rocky a doggy cookie, and then he goes and lies on his bed until somebody needs him. Sometimes the children are really scared, and sometimes they're crying, and then the nurse calls Rocky to come and help them be calm. He plays with them in the waiting room, or he may even go into the room where the doctor will see them."

"Yes," Mama said, "Tyler told me about Rocky, too. He was really excited about it! Rocky is a good example of what is called a 'service dog.'"

"Dogs help in other ways, too," Daddy started to speak. "I saw dogs herding sheep when I went to Australia."

"Oh, I saw that too, at the fair!" said Chris. "The dog even walks on the backs of the sheep!"

Emma spoke up again. "In my nature magazine, there was a story about dogs finding lost people. Sometimes they dig humans out of the snow. Or if a child gets lost, the dog can smell the child's clothes and then go searching for him or her."

Mama added, "You know, dogs are also used to find people after a bad earthquake, or any other time when buildings fall down."

"Dogs like bloodhounds go hunting for escaped criminals, too," Chris added.

Thinking about another service dog she had seen, Mama said, "One time I was on a long trip to see Grandpa G, and I was riding the bus. On the way, the bus had a problem. When we got to the next town, the driver stopped at a McDonalds – or a Burger King, or someplace like that. He told all of us passengers to just rest there and get some food if we wanted to, and that he would be back in an hour or two, after he got the bus fixed. A lot of us just waited outside."

Mama continued, "One lady was sitting on the grass beside the sidewalk, and lying right beside her was a middle-sized dog wearing a special vest with a leash on it. I started visiting with the woman, and after a while I asked about her dog. She told me that she had a health problem called epilepsy, which sometimes gave her seizures. A bad seizure could make her fall down and start shaking all over, so much so that she could get hurt really badly.

"As a little puppy, her dog had been taught to know when a person's seizure was about to happen! Somehow it was able to let her know that it was time to sit or lie down so that she would be safe."

"My teacher said that service dogs are not pets," Emma said. "They're just working dogs."

"That's right," said Daddy. "Their job is to help their owner in whatever way is needed. You've all thought of a lot of good ways that dogs can help people. Do you know why dogs can be so good at all those different things?"

After a short silence, Mama answered, "Because they are loyal and faithful to their owners."

"What does 'loyal' mean?" Danielle wanted to know.

"Being loyal, or having loyalty, is kind of like a glue or strong tape that holds two people's hearts together in love and caring," Daddy told her. "Think of it like this. You have a friend: you like that person, and even if they have a really bad day or get sick, you are still friends. That's loyal."

Mama said. "One of my friends said that loyalty is like how even if you forget to feed your dog, or you yell at him, he will still be your friend. That loyalty is what makes dogs man's best friend."

Then Daddy asked Chris and Emma, "Do you remember when Danni was born? How did Colonel act?"

"Danni cried too much, and Colonel didn't like all the noise!" Chris answered immediately.

Danielle made a face at Chris, then asked Mama, "Did I really cry a lot, Mommy?"

"Well, not too much, Danni. But it is true that Colonel didn't like the noise when you cried. There was something else that bothered him, though. Colonel knew Daddy and Chris and Emma and me. He also knew all our friends who came to visit."

"If any strangers came around, he really barked a lot," Emma added.

"Yes," Mama continued. "Colonel always protected our family. But Danielle was a newcomer; a stranger to him. I worried for quite a few weeks about how he would act toward Danielle. I was a little afraid that I might not be able to trust him completely.

"Then one day I walked outside carrying her in my arms. Colonel greeted me in his usual way. Do you remember what that was? Whenever I went outside, Colonel would very, very gently take my wrist in his mouth. But he never bit hard enough to hurt me. It was just his way of saying, 'Hi, I'm glad you've come outside to see me.'"

"Sometimes he did that to me, too," Emma said.

Mama continued, "So that day, after saying hi to me, he reached up and gently took Danielle's hand in his mouth. I am sure it was his way of saying, 'Okay, new baby: I understand that you are part of my family now.' From then on I knew that Colonel would protect Danielle and be careful with her as a part of our family."

Daddy spoke up. "All these dogs – the guard dogs, the guide dogs for the blind, the search-and-rescue dogs, and all the other working dogs – know their master. They have learned to respect and obey that owner, and they will stay by that person, protecting their master, no matter what happens.

"Just like these loyal dogs, boys and girls – and big people, too – should always be loyal to their family."

Mama looked at Chris, then at Emma and Danielle. "Do you know what it means to be loyal to your family?" she asked.

"Showing respect for your parents," Emma suggested.

"Loving them and taking care of them," said Chris.

Mama asked, "Do you mean loving your parents even though we do things you don't like? Even though we have to punish you sometimes?"

The children nodded their heads, and Mama continued, "It's just like how we still love each one of you children even when you act bad. We may not like what you *do*, but we still love *you*."

"There are other things that loyalty means, too," Daddy added. "Like being thankful, and showing appreciation when someone does something for you."

"And not saying bad things about your family when you are talking with other people," Chris suggested.

"Also, helping them when they need your help," said Emma.

"I'll even take care of you when you get old!" little Danielle said, and she quickly went and hugged both Daddy and Mama.

Loyalty

A dog, they say, is man's best friend,
And he'll be faithful to the end.
That's how children should be, too:
Always loving, loyal, and true.

Squawky Cocky

"Mommy, Daddy, come outside quickly!" called Danielle one Sunday morning. "Hurry, hurry, before they go away!"

Wondering what all the excitement was about, Mama and Daddy rushed out the door and down the steps.

"Look, Mommy, up there! What kind of birds are those?" Danielle pointed excitedly to where four beautiful white birds were perched high up in a tree. They were very pretty to look at … but their voices sounded like angry children screaming at each other.

"Those are cockatoos," Mama answered.

While Mama, Daddy, and Danielle watched, three of the cockatoos flew to the next tree. "Look," Daddy said, pointing to one of the birds. "That one has a string – or a chain? – on its leg."

The birds flew from one tree to another. Finally they went out of sight, but Danielle could still hear them screeching. For several weeks after that, the cockatoos returned to the tall trees around the family house. Sometimes she saw them; other times she only heard their noisy calls.

One morning Daddy went to the park near their house to go jogging. As he got close to the park, he heard a terrible screeching. The noise was coming from high up in a very tall tree. Looking up, he saw the cockatoo with the chain on its leg. That chain was caught tightly; the bird could not get loose.

Daddy wanted to help that poor helpless cockatoo, but the tree was much too tall, so there was nothing he could do. But later on, when he went by the tree again, he was very happy to see that somehow the bird seemed to have gotten free from the tree.

> *As he got close to the park, he heard a terrible screeching.*

For the next few weeks, no one thought much about the cockatoos. Then, early one morning when Mama and Daddy were walking to the park together to exercise, they saw a big, white cockatoo on the driveway near his office, which was just across the street from the park.

Mama walked slowly toward the bird. It screeched at her, and she really jumped! But she slowly stepped a little closer. Then she noticed the chain around its leg, and realized that this must be the same bird that they'd seen earlier. The bird tried to get away from Mama, but it seemed like it was too hurt and weak to move more than a few inches, so it just screeched again.

Mama could see that the cockatoo needed help, but she was afraid to catch it with her bare hands. Daddy gave her his t-shirt to hold the bird with, but even then, she was afraid that it would bite or peck at her, so she went home and brought back a small cage. It was for hamsters, but she explained to Daddy that maybe she could put the top carefully over the cockatoo, then gently slide the bottom under the bird and carry it back home that way.

When Mama tried to get the poor hurt cockatoo into the cage, it squawked and screeched so loudly that she thought she would go deaf! But finally she caught it, and she took it back to the house while Daddy went jogging.

Ebony, their little black kitten, met Mama near the door. She was very curious and tried to come close to the cage. But the cockatoo suddenly looked at the cat and gave one very loud "*Screeeeeeech!*" Poor frightened little Ebony ran away as fast as her kitten legs could carry her!

When Danielle and Emma saw the cockatoo, they could hardly believe their eyes, they were so excited. Even Chris, who always teased the girls about all of their pets, was very interested in this one.

Mama tried to feed the cockatoo some seeds, then fruit, and she also gave it water, but the poor bird seemed too sick to take anything at all. Finally, when Mama finished work for the day, she took it to the animal hospital.

When the veterinarian looked at the cockatoo, she told Mama, "The leg is badly swollen and infected, and this chain has to be taken off. We will have to give the bird anesthesia to make it sleep while we remove it." Then the doctor added, "But the cockatoo is so weak that I am afraid it may die during the operation. Do you still want us to try?"

Mama was sad to think that the bird might die, but she knew that it was so sick that they must do something for it, and soon! "Yes," Mama said. Then she went back home and waited for a call from the animal hospital.

When the telephone finally rang, it was good news: the chain was off, and the cockatoo was alive. Mama could go back to get her new pet.

At first, Daddy and Emma insisted that they should let the bird go free as soon as its leg was healed. Mama asked the veterinarian what would be best.

"If the bird imprints on you, it will not be able to live in the wild," the doctor told her.

Mama did not quite understand what was meant by "imprint."

"Well," the doctor explained, "if the bird does not like you, it will be able to go back into the wild. But if it really starts to love you, it would miss you too much if you were to send it away. In that case it would probably die."

Mama and Daddy decided to wait and see how the bird got along. Several times every day, Mama fed the cockatoo from her hand (Daddy and the children sometimes fed him sunflower seeds or pieces of fruit, but Mama was the only one the bird really trusted).

Meanwhile, everyone tried to think of a name. Chris had all sorts of funny ideas that Emma and Danielle didn't like, and he didn't like the names that they suggested. The problem was finally solved when Uncle Russell came to visit one evening. He watched the cockatoo put up the bright yellow crest feathers on its head and fuss whenever anyone except Mama walked near the cage. "You're a cocky old fellow," Uncle Russell told the bird. "I think that's a good name for you: 'Cocky.'"

Everyone agreed at once. Their sassy, sulfur-crested cockatoo would be called "Cocky." But even though the whole family liked Cocky, he was still Mama's bird.

Over time she began trying to rub and scratch the back of his head. He certainly did enjoy that! He would turn his head to one side so Mama could scratch his neck, and he would move closer and closer, begging for more love.

Meanwhile, Cocky's leg finally healed enough that he could hold food in his sharp claws while he ate. But several months later, he still limped very badly when he tried to move around the large birdcage that Mama had gotten for him.

One day, after Mama finished cleaning his cage, she left the door open to see what Cocky would do. In a little while, Cocky climbed out onto the top of it. Mama watched carefully, and after a few minutes, she gently picked him up and put him back inside.

Weeks and months went by. Cocky enjoyed having the family eat all their meals at the table near his cage. He began to squawk for food every time anyone sat down, so that during dinner it seemed like no one sat still for very long. As soon as Cocky called, Danielle would jump up to give him an almond. Sometimes Chris would feed him a slice of orange, or Emma would rush to hand him some rice or bread. Daddy's arm was long enough that he could just turn around and reach from his chair to offer "Squawky Cocky" something to eat.

Everyone liked Cocky, and Cocky loved all the attention.

One evening when the children were all in bed, Mama was ironing clothes near the big cage. Cocky came as close to Mama as he could get and started calling to her. Mama turned around, opened the cage, and reached in to scratch his head for a while. Then she decided to leave the cage door open. Cocky did not waste any time getting out. He climbed onto the top of the cage and sat there.

When Mama finished ironing, it was time to put him back into the cage. But this time, Cocky did not want to go back in! He liked being more free. When Mama tried to pick him up, he flew to the next room and grabbed onto the curtains with his sharp claws. She tried to catch him, and he flew away again. Mama began to worry that Cocky might get hurt. She had seen birds fly into windows or mirrors and break their necks, and she certainly did not want that to happen to Cocky. But he did not want to obey.

Slowly, slowly, she walked toward Cocky, talking softly to him. Very slowly she moved her hands toward him. Finally she put one hand on his back ... then she put her other hand on his chest ... and she held on to him.

But Cocky still did not want to go anywhere, so he bit her finger. Ouch! That hurt, but Mama would not let go. Cocky bit harder. *Ohh*, was that painful! Still Mama held on, hurrying toward the cage, putting him inside, and locking the door. Her finger was bleeding, and it kept hurting for several days, but at least Cocky was safe again.

☙ ✤ ❧

You know, Cocky reminds me of some children I know. All of us have rules that we must obey. Many of those rules are meant to help us to be better people; to be honest and kind. Other rules are to keep us safe, like rules about crossing streets, not playing with fire or firecrackers, and not talking to strangers.

But sometimes boys and girls cry or get angry when Mother or Father or Teacher or someone else makes them obey the rules. Like Cocky, they want to bite back with angry words or actions. They don't think about how they might get hurt if they disobey. They just want more freedom to do whatever they want to do!

Remember, though: rules are meant to keep us *free*. Free from harm and danger; free from hurt and ruined lives. Free to be happy and healthy.

When God made this earth and the people in it, He gave us some very important rules to follow. Later God even wrote them down on two pieces of stone with His own finger. These are the ten rules that He wrote, and they are called the Ten Commandments:

1. Do not have any other Gods but the one God in Heaven who made you.
2. Do not make any idols but only worship God.
3. Always use God's name with respect.
4. Remember to keep the Sabbath as a special holy day. You may do all your work in six days, but the seventh day is to worship God.
5. Honor, respect and obey your father and your mother.
6. Be kind to others, and do not kill or hurt anyone.
7. Keep your promise to always love and be loyal to your husband or wife.
8. Do not steal or take anything that does not belong to you.
9. Always tell the truth.
10. Do not be jealous or want something that belongs to someone else.

All of these rules really just mean two things:

First, that we should love the Lord our God with all our hearts.

Second, that we should love other people and be good and kind to everyone.

That is how we can live the happiest lives.

Acey's Gift

"Wow, do I ever have a story to tell you all about our Acey-cat!" Mama told the children one evening. "You know how lots of aunts and uncles and cousins and friends are coming this weekend for Grandma Johnson's memorial service? Because of that, we are going to be feeding lots and lots of people, both at home for a few days and at the church after the service. That's why, while you were all out with Daddy for the day, I had to spend a long time in town shopping."

Mama continued, "I came home with *lots* of groceries, so the car was really full. There were bags and boxes everywhere: on the back seat, the front seat, and covering the floor of the car. There was just barely enough room for me to sit and drive! Even the trunk was packed.

"When I got home, I started unloading everything I'd bought. First I brought in the fruit, vegetables, and other cold food so I could put it into the refrigerator right away. Then I brought in all the canned and packaged food. Finally, I started bringing in things from the trunk. There were paper towels, toilet paper, napkins, paper plates and cups, plastic spoons and forks, and so much more.

> *I pulled the box toward me from the back of the trunk so I could look inside. But – uh- oh – it wasn't empty!*

"While I was emptying the trunk, I just left the lid open. I didn't think there was any need to close and reopen it every time I came back for more. Two or three times I found Acey-cat in there, and each time I would wave my arm and shoo her out.

"Finally the trunk was empty, except for the big shoe box that I always keep in there to hold little things so they won't roll or slide around. I went out one last time, just to make sure I hadn't left anything in that box.

"Well, Acey-cat had jumped inside it while I was in the house. She once again hopped down from the car when she saw me coming. I pulled the box toward me from the back of the trunk so I could look inside. But – uh- oh – it wasn't empty! What do you think was inside?"

"Some baby kittens?" asked Danielle excitedly.

"No," Mama answered, "it was a freshly-killed gopher!"

"Oh, gross!" Emma groaned.

"You know how Acey always likes to bring gophers or birds she has caught and killed, and leave them on the mat near one of the doors?" Mama went on. "This time she decided that the perfect place to put her little present was right where I was working, so I could see what a good cat she had been!"

The children all laughed.

"Do you know what I did with it? I threw it across the creek behind the house, into the grass where I wouldn't have to see it again!" Mama said. "Later in the day I started to think that maybe the dead gopher in that box in the trunk was Acey's gift of love for me. But do you think I was thankful for it when I found it? Did I like and appreciate her gift?" Mama asked.

"No way!" Chris answered. Emma and Danielle both shook their heads.

"Not at all," Mama agreed.

"But if it was her gift of love, Mommy, that wasn't nice of you," Danielle scolded.

"I know, Danni," Mama said. "When I started thinking about the dead gopher being Acey's love gift, it really made me stop and consider. God has given us some special gifts of love, too. They are *not* presents that came wrapped up in pretty paper and ribbons, but something much, much better than that. Can you tell me what some of His gifts are?"

"The Bible?" asked Chris.

"Yes, Chris," answered Mama. "That is a very special gift to tell us how much He loves us, and to tell us how to live."

"Jesus," said Emma.

"Oh, for sure," said Mama. "Jesus was the most wonderful gift, because He came to live here on earth with us; to save us from sin so we can go to Heaven someday and live with Him."

Daddy finally spoke up, "We have to choose what we are going to do with God's gifts, though. We could just reject them and throw them away. What are ways that might happen?"

"By not reading our Bible," answered Chris.

"Or not listening carefully to Bible stories when Daddy reads them, right Danni?" asked Mama.

Danielle nodded *yes*.

"By not loving and obeying Jesus, but letting Satan make us do bad things," Emma said.

"You know," Mama said, "this all makes me think of how we got Acey-cat to start with. When Auntie Sydney was away at college, she was working in the Ace Hardware store during her summer vacation. One day a lady came into the store with a box carrying three tiny little kittens. She told Auntie Sydney and the other people working there that she had found them up at the college airport. Some unkind person had just left them there, rejected! Not wanted."

"That was so mean!" poor little Danielle cried.

"You are so right, Danni," Mama told her. "Auntie Sydney quickly told the lady that she might be able to take one of the kittens. She asked her to wait a minute while she phoned Grandma Johnson to ask if it would be okay for the kitten to live at Grandma's farm when school started again. Well, Grandma Johnson said that would be fine. So Auntie Sydney chose one from the box and took it home with her that evening; and she named it "Ace" because of where she had gotten it.

"That little kitten started following Auntie Sydney around like she was its mama. It would tag along behind her from one room to another. It would go outside with her. Would you believe that little Acey-kitten even went into the shower with her?!"

"Really?" both Emma and Danielle asked in surprise.

"I saw it with my very own eyes, more than once!" Mama laughed. "By the time school started and Acey had to go to Grandma Johnson's farm, we had already moved there, ourselves. So Acey ended up being our cat instead of Grandma's. Then she followed *me* everywhere!

"If I was sitting on the sofa with papers filling my lap, it didn't matter to Acey. She would jump up and sit in the middle of everything. At night, she jumped onto my bed and curled up between my legs. When I was sewing, she would be right in the middle of my work. If I was building a fire in the wood stove, she was underfoot. Even in the car, Acey wanted to be either in my lap or on my shoulder, licking my neck!"

"Ooh, that must have tickled!" giggled Danielle.

"It did for a while," Mama said. "But after twenty or thirty minutes, my neck would start to get sore, because her tongue was so rough!

"I think that Acey is one of God's gifts to me," Mama continued. "She has taught me some important lessons. For example, just like how Acey always wanted to be with Auntie Sydney or me, God really wants us to be with Him. That's why He sent Jesus to this earth and called Him 'Emmanuel.' Do you know what that name means, Chris?"

"God with us," he answered.

"Right. Jesus came to be with the people that He made and loved," said Mama. "Then He took the punishment for our sins by dying on a cross; because the Bible says that the wages, or payment, for sin is death. That's found in the Bible in the book of Romans, chapter six and verse twenty-three. Afterward, God made Jesus live again and took Him up to Heaven. Now Jesus is there making a beautiful place for us all to live; a place where no one will ever be sad or hurt or sick again. No one will ever die there."

"But to go to Heaven, we have to make a very important choice," Daddy said. "If we choose to not accept or to throw away God's gift of Jesus coming to earth to live and die for our sins, like Mama threw away Acey's gopher, then we will waste the most important gift ever. But if we choose to receive Jesus and all of God's special gifts, they are just waiting for us to accept them. Even more than Acey wanted to be with Auntie Sydney or Mama, Jesus wants very, very much to be with us."

"That's right," Mama said. "We can be *so* thankful that Jesus loves us the way He does and has given us such wonderful gifts. We should be happy for all the stories in the Bible. We can be happy to let Jesus help us to always do what is right. And we can be very happy to love Jesus back, to pray, and to sing about His love."

Sweet or Stinky?

"Mama, have you been over to Auntie Doe's house since we got back from vacation?" Emma asked.

"Not yet," Mama answered. "I'll be going over in a little while to see if everything is okay, since they are still on vacation too. Why do you ask?"

"There's a big hole in her flower garden," said Emma, "and there's dirt and sand all over the sidewalk and porch!"

Danielle was curious now. "Let's go see it, Mommy!" she said.

So Mama went to the cupboard, where she kept the keys for the house next door, and invited Danielle and Emma to walk with her. When they got there, she exclaimed, "Oh my, what a mess! We'd better get the broom and sweep this clean before Auntie Doe and Uncle Bob get home tonight."

"Who made this mess, Mama?" Emma asked. "It's a lot bigger than the gopher holes out in the field."

"It certainly is. You know, I think it might have been a skunk," Mama answered. "We have seen them around a few times."

"And sometimes we *smell* them at night!" Danielle wrinkled up her nose as she remembered.

"That's true," said Mama. "Do you know why we usually just smell them at night?"

"Because they are 'nocturnal' animals," Emma answered. "That means they are awake at night."

"That's right, Emma," Mama said. "By the way, did you know that skunks are good diggers, with long 'toenails' on their very strong front feet? That way they can dig for earthworms and other little animals that live underground; and if they don't find a good hollow log or a big hole in a tree to live in, they will dig their own 'burrow,' which is a tunnel in the ground."

About that time Chris walked over and wondered aloud what Mama and the girls were looking at. When they showed him the burrow in the flower bed, he asked Danielle, "Do you know what they eat, Danni?"

Danielle shook her head and said, "No, what? Is it something yummy?"

"Beetles, mice and rats, grasshoppers, birds' eggs, and mushrooms," Chris told her. "They sometimes eat fruit and berries," he said, then teased his little sister with, "but they *really* like frogs!"

"No wonder we have skunks so close by this year!" exclaimed Emma. "We had thousands of pollywogs – tadpoles – in the pond this spring. So now we've got all those cute little frogs everywhere."

"There are lots of grasshoppers this summer, too," added Mama.

"Remember when Benji and his little brother came here with their Daddy one day?" Danielle asked. "They were trying to catch grasshoppers and put them into a little cage. It was funny when one of the grasshoppers got out inside their car! Benji had to chase it until it finally hopped out of the car."

> *Oh, dear! There, on the empty concrete floor, was a big problem.*

"It sounds like you had some fun," Mama told Danielle. Then she continued, "I think that while we were all gone for vacation this summer, the skunk found that everything was quiet and safe; so he just moved right in and made himself at home!"

Having cleaned up outside of Auntie Doe's house, everyone walked back home together.

Later that evening, Mama remembered something that had happened a few years earlier, and started telling the children a story.

"I remember a kind of scary thing that happened to Auntie Sydney and me when she was just about your age, Emma," Mama began. "She was staying here at the farm with Daddy and me while Grandma Johnson was back east with Daddy's brother and his family.

"One evening I was in the house while Sydney was outside playing. I wasn't worried about her getting hurt or into trouble, so I was just doing some work. After a while she came in for supper, then we took our baths, had our worship, and went to bed.

"The next morning when I went out to the carport …. Oh, dear! There, on the empty concrete floor, was a *big* problem. You see," Mama went on, "while Sydney had been playing out there the night before, she had set the cage trap. And what do you think was caught inside of it?"

"A porcupine?" asked Danielle.

"No, not a porcupine," Mama answered. "We had raccoons and deer at the farm, but porcupines don't live in that area."

"A skunk!" Chris and Emma guessed together.

"That's right, a very cute little skunk!" said Mama. She explained, "Grandma Johnson had used that cage trap many times to catch the raccoons that caused so much trouble with the fruit trees. She would take trapped raccoons a few miles away in her car, stop, and open the cage door to set them free in a new place.

"Grandma finally learned that if she set the trap up on that long work table out on the carport, she could catch raccoons. But if she set the trap on the floor, she would probably catch a skunk instead. Auntie Sydney didn't know that, though, so she just set the trap right on the concrete."

"Oh, no!" Danielle started to worry. "How did you get it out, Mommy?"

"Well, that was a real problem, Danni. I knew for sure that I did not want to get sprayed by the skunk!" Mama answered. "So I got one of those great big, black plastic garbage bags. Then I got the scissors, and I cut one side and the end of the bag and wrapped it around my waist to protect myself. But there was a problem with this idea: the plastic made noise whenever I moved, and this scared the poor little skunk.

"The next big problem was that I could not figure out how to open the cage! Each time I tried, the little skunk, which was in the other end of it, started to tap his front feet. *Uh-oh!* I thought. That was a big warning signal."

Emma now started to be afraid, wondering how Mama was going to get out of the danger. She had heard enough about skunks to know that the next thing after stomping would be a raised tail. "So what did you do?" she asked Mama.

"Well, I decided I'd better phone Grandma Johnson and ask her how to open the cage door," Mama answered. "She explained it to me very carefully. And, believe me, I *listened* carefully. I really did not want to get sprayed by that little skunk!

"After hearing Grandma's instructions, the first thing I did was to throw away that plastic garbage bag 'apron' I'd been using. Then I got a little bit of bread and fruit out of the refrigerator, came back out, and walked slowly to the end of the cage where the little skunk was standing. I moved very, *very* slowly so that I wouldn't scare him. I put the food through the bars of the cage and *slowly* moved back to the other end of the cage.

"Carefully, quietly I worked, and finally the cage door was open. *Yay!* At last I was safe! I could get away and let that little skunk come out whenever he wanted to," Mama said happily.

"Wow! That must have been really scary!" said Emma.

Daddy had come into the house and he heard the last part of the story. "I'd say that God was really taking care of your mother!" he said. "If she had gotten sprayed, she would have been STINKY for a long time! My friend Ralph told me that one time a skunk sprayed just outside their bedroom. The window was open, so the smell came right into the house … and into their clothes closet!

"Two or three months later, they drove to the town where his sister lived," Daddy continued. "They got there just in time to go to church with her and her family. They walked in and sat down, and after a minute or two, his sister turned toward him, sniffed a bit, and whispered, 'Did you hit a skunk on your way here this morning?' He told her no, then remembered the skunk by their bedroom window. They had gotten used to the smell after a few days, but the odor was still in their clothes!"

"I'm sure glad Mama's skunk didn't get her!" Emma said.

"You know," Daddy said, "these skunk stories make me think of the Bible verse in the second book of Corinthians, the second chapter, verses fourteen and fifteen. It says that we can really thank God for showing us how to live and share the message of His love everywhere, which is just like a sweet-smelling perfume. Our offering, our gift to God, should be like a perfume that goes to everyone around us."

"Sometimes we act stinky," Mother said. "Like if we are selfish or mean, or if we don't obey. There are lots of ways we can stink worse than I would have if that little skunk had sprayed me!"

"But there are also many ways we can smell sweet, aren't there?" Daddy asked the children. "What ways can you think of?"

"Being good," Danielle was quick to answer.

"Obeying and being kind," Emma added. "And sharing what we have with others."

"Chris, what do you think?" Daddy asked him.

"Being helpful. Or being polite," he answered.

"And being cheerful," Mama added. "I read something very good a while back. It said that morning, noon, and night – that means all the time – we should be thankful: that this would be like a sweet perfume to Jesus, who has given us *so* many good things."

Daddy added, "The Bible also tells us in Galatians, chapter five, verses twenty-two and twenty-three, that if we have God's Holy Spirit in our lives, we will have love, joy, peace, patience, kindness, goodness, faithfulness, gentleness, and self-control. Now, what happens if Mother sprays some perfume on her neck?" he asked.

"We can smell her when she walks by us!" Chris laughed.

"That's right," Daddy said. "And when we really have the love of Jesus in our hearts, we can't hide it: everyone around us will know about it."

Where Are You?

Mama asked the children, "Do you remember when I went to our cabin in Maine last October? The autumn leaves were so beautiful that I really didn't spend much time at the cabin except at night! I spent most of my time either in the car or out taking pictures of all the beauty.

"One day while I was out driving around, I went to our church summer camp, where your cousin Gracie has worked as a lifeguard for several summers. It is a really nice place with a very pretty lake. I walked down to the platform where Gracie would work during the warmer months, imagining how she watched carefully whenever anyone was in the water. But I was scared to climb the ladder way up to where she would sit in order to better see if someone was having trouble swimming in the icy-cold water."

"I remember Gracie telling us how freezing cold that lake is, even in the summer," said Chris. "Brr, I don't think I'd want to swim there!"

"Me neither," said Emma.

"Well," Mama said, "while I was looking at the lake and taking pictures of all the red, orange, and yellow maple trees on the far side of the lake, I saw a type of bird that I had never seen before. I started trying to take pictures of it, but that was harder than I expected. That bird would swim or float along just long enough for me to get my camera ready, then it would suddenly disappear!"

"Where did it go, Mommy?" Danielle wanted to know.

"It was diving under the water, Danni," Mama answered. "And it would stay down for a *long* time! It did that again and again, but I did finally get one pretty good picture of it."

"What was it doing, Mommy?" Danielle asked.

"I guessed that it was probably looking for food," Mama answered, "but really I didn't know, any more than I knew what kind of bird it was, or anything else about it.

"So when I got back to the cabin that evening, I looked in my bird book and on the internet to see what I could find out. I learned that it was a common loon, and it lives mostly in the north where it is colder. It was diving to find fish for its dinner, since that's what it always likes to eat. I also learned that loons are pretty good fliers, but it can take them a long distance to get started."

"Why do they need such a long way?" Emma asked.

"Probably because they are quite big birds, and they have great big feet. Loons are sort of like large, heavy airplanes, which also need a long runway in order to take off. Loons' big feet also make them really good swimmers, though."

"Sort of like they're always wearing fins!" Chris joked.

"Yes, I guess so, Chris," Mama smiled. "However, those big feet make it hard for the loons to walk very well on the land. Even so, they do build their nests on land: out of grass, mud, twigs, and weeds from underwater."

"That doesn't sound like a very soft nest," Emma said.

"I suppose not, but the grass probably makes it softer," said Mama. "Father loon chooses where the nest will be, but both the mother and father work on building it. And their nests are always very close to the water, so they can quickly dive in if an enemy comes."

"If they are big birds, who are their enemies?" asked Emma.

"Well," answered Mama, "on land, they have to worry about raccoons, weasels, and skunks. There are also bigger birds, like bald eagles and ospreys. Even crows, ravens, or seagulls may attack them or take their eggs or baby chicks. In the water, there may be otters, snapping turtles, or even big fish that might like to eat an egg or a chick.

"Once the eggs are laid," Mama continued, "the parents take turns sitting on them until they hatch. Baby loons can swim and dive very soon after hatching, but since they live where it is very cold, for the first two weeks, they mostly ride on their parents' backs to keep warm."

"That sounds like fun! It's like a piggy-back ride," Danielle giggled.

"Mostly I think it's just warmer and safer," Daddy spoke up.

Mama said, "One of the parents will bring the babies little fish to eat. Then, when the chicks are about six weeks old, they will go fishing for themselves.

"Loons make four different kinds of sounds," Mama went on. "If either the mama or daddy loon senses that there is danger, it will usually make a noise that tells the others to be careful. If the father thinks that there is some really terrible danger, though, he will screech very loudly. But if everything is fine, most often they just 'talk' to each other with sounds sort of like, '*whoohh-whoohh-whoohh*,' kind of like how an owl hoots. That call really says, 'Where are you?' The other loons usually answer back with the same sound.

"Here's another story about loons. One day while I was in Maine, our neighbor Judy and I went shopping together," Mama said. "At one of the stores, I was looking at some stuffed animals, wondering if there were any that I could use when I tell stories to the kindergarten class at your school. There was a cute little stuffed bird that looked very real. But I couldn't think of any stories to use it for."

"I like it when you come to my class!" Danielle said, smiling at Mama.

"So do I, Danni," Mama said. "I showed Judy the little bird and I told her why I was looking at the stuffed animals. Then *she* told *me* a story: about when she and Bob went on a camping trip with their children.

"They had camped right near another pretty lake, way up north where it gets very cold. That's the kind of place that loons like to live; and a family of loons had built a nest not far from where Bob and Judy had pitched their tent. Judy told me that the first night they were there, the mama loon kept calling. It was like she was asking, 'Where are you?' But there was never any answer. So the mother just kept calling and calling. All night long Judy kept hearing, 'Where are you? … Where are you? … Where are you?'"

"Do you know what that makes me think of?" Daddy asked.

"What?" asked Danielle.

"In the Bible, in the book of Genesis, chapter three," Daddy began, "we can read the story about when God made the first man and woman, Adam and Eve. God told them that they could eat the fruit from every tree in the whole garden except just one. That one tree was a test to see if they loved God enough to obey Him."

"Oh, I know that story!" Danielle said excitedly. "But Eve went to that one tree that she wasn't supposed to go to, and there was a pretty snake that talked to her!"

"That's right," Mama told her, "but that was not just any common snake, was it?"

Danielle shook her head. "No! It was really Satan trying to make Eve be bad."

"Yes, it was, Danni. And she listened to him, and she took the fruit and ate it, didn't she?" Mama asked. "Then she went and shared the fruit with Adam. Sharing is fine if it is something good, but sharing can be very bad if it is something we aren't supposed to have or do, right?"

Danielle nodded.

"So Emma, what happened after Adam had eaten the fruit, too?" Daddy asked.

"They were afraid, so they went and hid in the bushes," she answered.

"That's right," Mama said. "Then God came along and asked, 'Where are you?' But didn't God know where they were?"

"Sure, He did," Chris spoke up. "God always knows where we are and what we are doing."

"That's right, Chris. But like Emma said, they were afraid of God because they had not obeyed Him," Daddy said. "Sometimes we aren't doing what we should be doing. Maybe we are not obeying those rules, the Ten Commandments, that God gave us.

"If we aren't doing what we should," Daddy continued, "if we are acting ugly like a cone shell, or stinky like a skunk, Jesus will keep calling us and asking, 'Where are you?' Maybe He will call through the voice of your teacher or your mother. Maybe He will use Grandma or Grandpa or me to call you to do what is right.

"We might be afraid, like Adam and Eve, but we must always remember that God loves us very much. He wants us to come to Heaven to live with Him forever, so God's Holy Spirit always keeps calling us to come back and follow Jesus; to listen to Him and obey Him."

The Crawling Carpet

One evening Daddy helped Mama bring an old, rolled-up carpet from the storage closet into the hall. He put it down on the floor and began to unroll it. That's when the excitement began, as suddenly a cockroach came running out of the carpet toward Mama!

Without thinking, she quickly stepped on it with her bare foot. "*Eww, awful!*" she groaned. Mama shivered as she thought about having smashed cockroach on the bottom of her heel. She was about to go get some tissue to clean it off when another one ran out of the carpet.

Daddy rushed to bring the vacuum cleaner. He plugged it in and turned on the switch. *Swoosh*, the vacuum sucked up one cockroach. Then another, and another. The more Mama and Daddy unrolled the carpet, the more cockroaches came running out. One or two of them flew for a few feet, trying to escape. Another one tried to squeeze through the tiny crack under the door. It would have gotten through, but Daddy caught it with the vacuum. By then Mama was ready with a shoe to kill any that Daddy missed.

At last the carpet was all unrolled, and all the cockroaches were vacuumed up. Just then, Danielle came into the room. "What are you doing, Mommy and Daddy?" she asked.

"You missed all the fun, Danni!" Daddy joked. "We've just been chasing cockroaches!"

"I want to see. Where are they?" Danielle asked, disappointed that she had missed any excitement.

"I hope they are all inside the vacuum cleaner," Mama sighed, "but there might be more inside the storage closet where the carpet came from."

Danielle hurried to the closet to look. She couldn't find any, but she did come back to Mama to ask, "Mommy, what are these things that look like little black beans?"

"Oh, no," Mama sighed. "I had better vacuum that closet very well, too." Then she answered Danielle's question: "Those are 'egg cases,' or 'egg capsules.' They're little sacks full of cockroach eggs. We must get rid of them, or we will have a *lot* of baby cockroaches. At least the little babies – called 'nymphs' – don't have any wings, so they can't fly. As they grow bigger, they molt, or shed their skin, as many as ten or twelve times. Finally, they grow up to be big cockroaches, running or flying around the house!"

Mama picked up an egg case from Danielle's hand and asked, "How many little nymphs do you think can hatch out of one of these, Danni?"

Danielle thought for a moment, then she answered, "Three?"

"No, more than that. One egg case has at least sixteen babies inside ... and it might have many more than that."

Danielle's eyes opened wide. "Really?" she asked.

"Truly," Mama answered. "On top of that, a mama cockroach only has to mate once in her life, and then she can lay one of those egg cases every month for about two years. That means that in her whole life, she could have hundreds or even thousands of new babies!"

Chris had walked into the room in time to hear the last few sentences. "Remember when we went to the big natural science museum in Washington, DC, with Grandma and Grandpa Johnson? Inside a glass case, they had a kitchen cupboard and some food. There were thousands and thousands of cockroaches in there. The sign there said that one mother and father could make as many as 20,000 more cockroaches in one year!"

"And to think," Mama exclaimed, "that there are 3,500 different kinds of these insects! I'm just thankful that not all of them live in houses. Still, we will have to be more careful to keep everything very clean so that we don't have any more cockroaches growing in our house.

"Of course, the only trouble is, cockroaches could come in with the food we bring back from the store. They could catch a free ride on your clothes or easily come in through the drains in the bathtub or sink. They love garbage cans, too!"

"Oh, yucky! They must be dirty." Danielle wrinkled up her face at that last thought.

"Yes, they are dirty, and they may be harmful to our health because they can carry germs on their bodies that may make us sick. When they crawl over our dishes or food, they can leave the germs behind. Later on, we may take in those germs when we eat."

"That reminds me of something very embarrassing that happened one time," Daddy finally spoke up. He gave Mama a funny look.

She knew right then what Daddy was talking about. "I remember," Mama nodded her head. "Dr. Lowry, Daddy's boss, came into town from his headquarters office in India, and Daddy invited him to our house for dinner."

Daddy continued with his story, "Emma set the table that evening with Mama's nice blue dishes that she only uses for very special occasions. But – uh-oh – Emma didn't rinse the plates or the matching glasses before putting them out. So when Dr. Lowry picked up his glass, there was a big, dead cockroach inside!"

"Oh, no!" Danielle exclaimed.

"Poor Mama was so embarrassed; her face turned really red!" Daddy added.

Mama smiled. She was quiet and thoughtful for a little while. Then she continued, "You know, I think we can learn something very important from the cockroaches. Where do they live?"

"In dirty places," Danielle answered.

"And what do they eat?" Mama asked.

Chris was the first to answer: "Garbage, and all the little bits of food they find on the floor or in the cupboards."

"Actually they will eat almost anything," Mama said. "Old plants, dead animals, spoiled fruit. They live on filthy, dirty stuff! And you know, some people are like that. They seem to be the happiest when they can find out bad things about other people. They gossip, telling all the bad things they have heard about someone. They may even talk badly about their friends!"

> *Instead of always looking for the darkness, like the cockroaches do, it would be so much better if we looked for the brightness in life.*

Mama paused for a moment, then she continued, "Instead of always looking for the darkness, like the cockroaches do, it would be so much better if we looked for the brightness in life. Look for the good things in other people and praise them, and learn to be thankful for the nice little things that others do for you."

"There's a really good verse about this in the Bible," Daddy said. "Philippians, chapter four, verse eight, tells us that whatever things are true, whatever things are honest, whatever things are fair, whatever things are pure and lovely, we should think about these things.

"Think about the beautiful, not the ugly," Daddy continued, "and think about all the things you can praise and thank God for and be happy about. Then you will be happier, and other people will be happy too."

☙ ❖ ❧

Look for the Rainbow

They say that you'll surely find in life
Exactly what you're looking for.
Cockroaches always look for dirtiness
In cupboards, in closets, or on the floor.

They come in through drains or under the door;
Or maybe in bags of food that you've brought
They eat dead animals or food that they find;
They like veggies or fruit that's starting to rot.

We think that's awful – we'd never eat those!
But people do something much worse than this:
They spend life looking for the bad all around,
And the beauty in life they seem to miss.

For some people it seems that nothing's just right.
If the food isn't perfect, they fuss and complain.
When raindrops fall, they wish there were sun;
If the sun is shining, they'd rather have rain.

If you look for something to grumble about,
Or you always like to criticize,
You'll find that there is bad everywhere –
It's sure to be there in front of your eyes.

But if you look for the good in others you know,
And you search for something to praise,
You'll find there's some good in everyone
And you'll find you have happier days.

As I heard a friend of mine once say,
Instead of grumbling and feeling low,
"If I were born on a rainy day,
I'd look in the sky for a pretty rainbow."

The Silvery Trail Makers

Early one morning Mama and Daddy decided to take the children for a walk in the park. The sidewalk and grass were still wet from the morning dew, and both had shiny, silver lines upon them here and there.

"What are those?" Danielle wondered out loud.

"They might be from a slug or a snail," Mama answered. "They are almost the same, except that the slug doesn't carry its house on its back, like the snail does with its shell."

As they walked farther, Chris found who their trail-maker was: a common, ordinary snail. He knelt down on one side of it, while Emma and Danielle stood on the other side. They watched as it seemed to slide very slowly across the sidewalk, leaving a ribbon of silver slime behind it. "Mom, why does he make that trail?" Chris asked.

"It's to make a smooth path for him to move on, Chris," Mama answered. "That way, the rough sand or rocks won't hurt him. Did you know that a snail can even crawl over broken glass or a sharp razor blade without being hurt? It's all because of that trail he makes."

"A razor blade? Wow!" Chris exclaimed. "I don't think I'd want to try that, even if I did have a slimy trail under me!"

They all kept watching the snail. At the edge of the sidewalk were many dried-up leaves and seed pods from a big tree nearby, but these didn't bother the snail. It just kept moving, slowly and smoothly, toward the grass.

Just like any curious boy, Chris wondered what the snail would do if he blocked its way. He was careful not to move quickly or hurt it as he gently put a curly seed pod right in front of the snail. No matter: up, up, up the snail moved over the pod, not slowing down for anything.

"I wonder what he'll do if I put this twig in front of him," Emma said to Daddy as she picked up a little stick about as big as Daddy's thumb. They all watched to find out.

The twig wasn't a problem either. The snail stopped for just a few moments to check the twig with its long antennae. "See what it's doing?" said Daddy. "Those are its 'tentacles.' It 'sees' with the ones above, although a snail really only sees light and dark. With the short pair of tentacles below those, it smells its food or senses directions."

Everyone thought it was funny how the snail could stretch those long feelers until they were nearly an inch long, or else squeeze them tightly until they were really tiny. After checking the twig carefully, the snail decided to keep moving ahead. Up, up, and over the top the snail moved.

"Hey, be careful!" Chris warned as the snail's shell started to rock dangerously back and forth.

"Oh, it looked like he was going to tip over!" Danielle exclaimed once the snail was safely on the other side.

The little silver trail stretched out behind the snail, on the leaves and twig it had crossed. Mama pointed at it. "No matter where that snail goes or how far it travels," she said, "the trail will still be there. Of course, a snail or slug won't travel too far or too fast. Even a very speedy one will crawl only twenty or thirty feet in a whole hour! That probably isn't even as far as from the front of our house to the back. But even so, that trail still follows the little snail."

☙ ❖ ❧

Did you know that boys and girls also leave a trail behind them?

Sometimes there might be a trail of water or mud from dirty feet, or a trail of toys not picked up after play, but those aren't the kind of trail I'm thinking about.

Whatever we do in life, or whatever we say: these are the trail which will always follow us. Our trail may be our "reputation" – what other people think of us – or it may be our "influence": the bad or good effect we have on those around us.

I hope your trail will always be like the snail's: as silvery and sparkling as the trails Chris, Emma and Danielle saw on the dew-wet grass that morning at the park.

Your Trail

Like the little garden snail
That leaves a silvery trail,
Your words and actions follow you
So make them honest, kind and true.

Thief in the Night

"Mommy, why are there so many bear things in the living room?" Danielle asked one day.

"Don't you remember, Danni, when the bear came and made such a mess?" Chris asked his little sister.

"No," she answered.

Emma laughed. "We've called that 'the year of the bear' ever since!"

"Let me start at the beginning," Mama said to Danielle. "You know that the olives are getting bigger on all the olive trees here on the farm. In just another month or two, it will be time for us all to go out and pick them." She thought for a moment. "I hope we get a lot this year. They didn't turn out well last year, so we didn't have any to share with our friends, and we didn't have very good ones for our family to eat. But three years ago," Mama continued, "we had lots and lots of olives on the trees. Uncle David and Auntie Sydney were living here at the farm with us then.

"Uncle David was a really good help with all the olive work that year. He picked and picked and picked some more, getting way up high in the trees where Daddy and I really can't reach.

"After a day of picking, Daddy would put all the olives into big buckets on the concrete driveway and fill up those buckets with water that had a special chemical 'medicine' mixed in."

Chris spoke up, "You sure can't eat them right off the tree. They're really bitter!"

"That's right, Chris. Don't ever let someone try to feed you a nice black olive right off the tree!" Mama laughed. "I remember fooling one or two of my friends that way when I was young. Anyway, Daddy left the olives in that special solution for a few hours, and then we had to start rinsing them with fresh water. For the first day or two, someone had to empty all the water out and fill the buckets with clean water every two or three hours. If we didn't do that, the olives would get soft and mushy. Then, after a few days of rinsing them, it was time to start adding lots of salt to the water.

"Well, in the year of the bear, there were seven or eight buckets all ready for the salt, and there were another thirteen or fourteen just starting to get rinsed. Since Uncle David was helping, he and Daddy took turns rinsing during the night.

"One night Daddy rinsed them all, set his alarm clock, and went to bed early. At about eleven o'clock that night, Uncle David went out to take his turn. *Hmm*, he thought: something was not right. He found dirt and grass in some of the buckets, and a big handful of olives on the driveway beside one of them. But he just did the work and went back to bed.

"In the middle of the night, Daddy got out of bed, put on his shoes, and went out once more to do the rinsing. But what was this?! One bucket was tipped over, and its olives were spilled out onto the driveway … and a second bucket was completely empty!

"The next morning," Mama continued, "Daddy told me about what had happened. He wondered what had made the mess. Was it a raccoon? A coyote? Certainly not a deer?"

"Daddy was really silly!" Emma told Danielle.

"He certainly was, Emma," Mama laughed as she continued her story. "Then, while we considered the mystery, I remembered that about ten years earlier a bear had broken down the screen door at Grandma Johnson's house next door to us to get onto her porch. It made a terrible mess then! So I told Daddy, 'It sounds like a bear to me.'"

"Do you know what Dad said?" Chris asked. "He just laughed at Mama and said, 'No, I think it must have been an elephant!'"

"The funny thing is," Mama said, "later that morning Auntie Melanee and your cousins, Alyssa and Tyler, came to have lunch with us, and Daddy told her all about the olive thief. Guess what Auntie Melanee said? 'It sounds like a bear's work!' Do you know what Daddy said to *her*?

Chris answered right away, "'It must have been an elephant!'"

Everybody laughed at Daddy.

Mama resumed her story. "That evening, Auntie Sydney and Uncle David went into town for a while. When they got back, they turned the corner onto the driveway, and – *surprise!* – there on the carport, walking right toward the buckets of olives, was a big, brown bear! But it got scared and ran away. Auntie Sydney and Uncle David came rushing into the house and announced, 'We found your thief!'"

Danielle's eyes opened very wide, but she didn't say anything, so Mama continued. "Two nights later, while we were sleeping, that big bear came back again. At that time there were two refrigerators on the carport, so we could bottle the olives and keep them cold once they were ready. In those refrigerators we also had lots of bags of dried fruit, which I had worked hard on and planned to share with your aunties and uncles. Guess what happened?"

> *When they got back, they turned the corner onto the driveway, and – surprise! – there on the carport, walking right toward the buckets of olives, was a big, brown bear!*

"A great big mess!" Chris was the first to answer.

Emma added, "He pulled bottles of olives and bags of dried fruit out of the fridge. The back yard and part of the carport had stuff all over!"

"That's right; it was a *real mess!*" Mama said. "I was pretty unhappy that the bear wasted all those dried peaches, apricots, and nectarines. I guess he enjoyed them, though. But we had a lot of cleaning up to do, didn't we?"

Emma and Chris both nodded, and then Chris spoke up. "Then Auntie Melanee found bear poo out in the field, and it was full of olive seeds!"

"We all went looking for paw prints," Emma added. "Alyssa was the first person to find one, just above the concrete driveway. Then we found some more in the mud."

"Well, Danni, we had to do something to keep the bear from coming back and stealing more food out of the refrigerators," Mama said. "So Uncle David hung a radio up on the carport, and Daddy turned it on really loud at night; and we left all the outside lights on. That worked fine for the first night, the second night, and the third night. In fact, it worked for about a week. By then, Daddy decided that the bear must have gone away, so he went back to leaving all the lights off at night and didn't turn on the radio anymore.

"Everything seemed okay … for a while," Mama continued. "Then 'Trouble' came back and made a *really* big mess; he almost emptied that refrigerator. We had to clean up the carport and back yard a second time! So Daddy turned the lights and radio back on, but by now, the bear wasn't afraid of the noise and lights. He came back again the next night.

There wasn't much food left in that refrigerator anymore, but he checked again. He turned it partway around and got muddy pawprints all over it and on the bathroom window. But remember, there was still another refrigerator on the carport. So Daddy got a big, wide strap to hold it closed … although I think the bear could have torn it right off. Also, at night, Daddy parked his car really close to the refrigerator, to try and keep the bear from getting near enough to open it. Now guess what happened a few nights later?"

"I know!" Chris was the first to answer. "The bear climbed up on Dad's car!"

"You're right," Mama said. "Daddy woke up and heard something that sounded like a cake pan banging on the floor. So he got up and quickly, quietly went to the door to the carport. Daddy opened it and – oh, my! –

that bear was *just* climbing down from the roof of his new car! There were muddy footprints on it and a dent in the roof, which did not make him happy at all.

"The next morning we moved that refrigerator into the storage building. I think that was the last time the bear came to visit."

"But we still have all the bear stuff that our aunt and cousins gave us that Christmas," Emma said. "I like the sign that says, 'Bear stories told here'!"

"I like the little red and brown pillow on the sofa," Danielle added.

"My favorite is the drawing of the bear that your cousin Gavin burned into a piece of wood," Mama said, then she thought for a moment. "You know," she said, "I think there are a lot of lessons we can learn from our bear visits.

"First of all, Daddy didn't believe me when I told him I thought it was a bear, and he didn't believe Auntie Melanee, either. There are some people who don't know about Jesus, or else don't believe in Him even if someone tells them. That is sad, because if they don't believe that He loves them and wants them to be with Him someday soon, they won't be able to go to Heaven.

"Secondly, just like we never knew when that bear would come back, the Bible says that no one except God knows what day or hour Jesus will come back to this earth to take us to Heaven. In the Bible, in the book of Matthew, chapter twenty-four, verses thirty-six and forty-three, it says that even the angels don't know when Jesus will return. That means it is really important for us to always love and obey God, so that we are always ready. It also says, 'Remember this: if the owner of the house knew what time a thief was coming, then the owner would be ready for him. The owner would watch and not let the thief enter his house.'[6]

Mama concluded, "Just like how we kept getting surprised by our bear thief that came for a few nights, the day when Jesus comes back will be a surprise: it will be like a thief that comes in the night.

"But if we love Him and are waiting for Him to come again, it will be a *very* happy surprise!"

---

[6] ICB.

TEACH Services, Inc.
P U B L I S H I N G

We invite you to view the complete
selection of titles we publish at:
www.TEACHServices.com

We encourage you to write us
with your thoughts about this,
or any other book we publish at:
info@TEACHServices.com

TEACH Services' titles may be purchased in
bulk quantities for educational, fund-raising,
business, or promotional use.
bulksales@TEACHServices.com

Finally, if you are interested in seeing
your own book in print, please contact us at:
publishing@TEACHServices.com

We are happy to review your manuscript at no charge.

www.ingramcontent.com/pod-product-compliance
Lightning Source LLC
Chambersburg PA
CBHW042133160426
43199CB00021B/2893